Artist: Francine Auger

A.M. Klein, 1909-1972.

# *Naïm Kattan*

Naïm Kattan was born in Baghdad, Iraq. He graduated in law, and in 1947 studied literature in Paris. He immigrated to Canada in 1954 and launched the *Bulletin du Cercle juif* in Montreal. Since his arrival, he has contributed to many newspapers and magazines and has participated in radio and television broadcasts here and in a number of other countries. In 1967 he became Head of the Writing and Publishing Section of the Canada Council. He is currently an associate professor in the Département d'études littéraires at the Université du Québec à Montréal [Department of Literary Studies at the University of Quebec in Montreal]. Novelist, short story writer, essayist, and critic, Mr. Kattan is the author of some 20 works. He is a member of the Académie des lettres du Québec and the Royal Society of Canada.

**The Translator: Edward Baxter**

Edward Baxter was born in Summerside, Prince Edward Island, and is a graduate of Mount Allison University and the University of Toronto. He taught French for many years in Ontario secondary schools and was Head of Modern Languages at Don Mills Collegiate in North York until his retirement in 1986. In 1980 he was appointed to a one-year term as the first Poet Laureate of the City of North York. His translations of Jules Verne's *Famille sans nom* (*Family Without a Name*) and *Pays des fourrures* (*The Fur Country*) were published by NC Press of Toronto.

THE QUEST LIBRARY
is edited by
Rhonda Bailey



Editorial correspondence:
Rhonda Bailey, Editorial Director
XYZ Publishing
P.O. Box 250
Lantzville BC
V0R 2H0
E-mail: xyzed@telus.net

**In the same collection**

Ven Begamudré, *Isaac Brock: Larger Than Life.*
Lynne Bowen, *Robert Dunsmuir: Laird of the Mines.*
Kate Braid, *Emily Carr: Rebel Artist.*
William Chalmers, *George Mercer Dawson: Geologist, Scientist, Explorer.*
Judith Fitzgerald, *Marshall McLuhan: Wise Guy.*
Stephen Eaton Hume, *Frederick Banting: Hero, Healer, Artist.*
Betty Keller, *Pauline Johnson: First Aboriginal Voice of Canada.*
Michelle Labrèche-Larouche, *Emma Albani: International Star.*
Dave Margoshes, *Tommy Douglas: Building the New Society.*
Raymond Plante, *Jacques Plante: Behind the Mask.*
T.F. Rigelhof, *George Grant: Redefining Canada.*
Arthur Slade, *John Diefenbaker. An Appointment with Destiny.*
John Wilson, *John Franklin: Traveller on Undiscovered Seas.*
John Wilson, *Norman Bethune: A Life of Passionate Conviction.*
Rachel Wyatt, *Agnes Macphail: Champion of the Underdog.*

# A.M. Klein

**Canadian Cataloguing in Publication Data**

Kattan, Naïm, 1928-

A.M. Klein: poet and prophet

(The quest library ; 13)

Translation of: A. M. Klein : la réconciliation des races et des religions
Includes bibliographical references and index.

ISBN 0-9688166-6-5

1. Klein, A.M. (Abraham Moses), 1909-1972. 2. Poets, Canadian (English) – Quebec (Province) – Montréal – Biography. 3. Jews – Quebec (Province) – Montréal – Biography. I. Title. II. Series : Quest library ; 13.

PS8521.L45Z7213 2001 C811'.52 C2001-941198-7
PS9521.L45Z7213 2001
PR9199.3.K53Z7213 2001

Legal Deposit: Fourth quarter 2001
National Library of Canada
Bibliothèque nationale du Québec

XYZ Publishing acknowledges the support of The Quest Library project by the Canadian Studies Program and the Book Publishing Industry Development Program (BPIDP) of the Department of Canadian Heritage. The opinions expressed do not necessarily reflect the views of the Government of Canada.

The publishers further acknowledge the financial support our publishing program receives from The Canada Council for the Arts, the ministère de la Culture et des Communications du Québec, and the Société de développement des entreprises culturelles.

Chronology: Michèle Vanasse
Index: Darcy Dunton
Layout: Édiscript enr.
Cover design: Zirval Design
Cover illustration: Francine Auger
Photo research: Anne-Marie Sicotte

XYZ Publishing
1781 Saint Hubert Street
Montreal, Quebec H2L 3Z1
Tel: (514) 525-2170
Fax: (514) 525-7537
E-mail: xyzed@mlink.net
Web site: www.xyzedit.com

Distributed by:
General Distribution Services
325 Humber College Boulevard
Toronto, Ontario M9W 7C3
Tel: (416) 213-1919
Fax: (416) 213-1917
E-mail: cservice@genpub.com

# A.M. KLEIN

THE QUEST LIBRARY

## POET AND PROPHET

Translation by Edward Baxter

# *Contents*

National Archives of Canada/PA-211142.

A.M. Klein's graduating class, Baron Byng High School (Klein is second from left in the second row from the bottom). At Baron Byng, Abe discovered a taste for literature, formed lasting friendships, and fell in love.

# 1

## *The Apprentice Years*

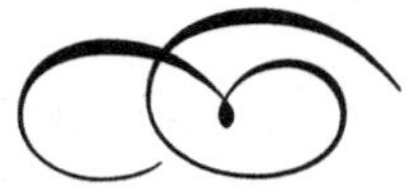

His full name was Abraham Moses Klein, but at home they called him by his nickname – Abe. When he was a child, his mother always lulled him to sleep with her songs. One night he was feverish and sleep would not come.

"I'm going to tell you a story," said his mother. "Your father and I used to live in a little village in Ukraine called Ratno, far, far away from Montreal. At that time the Jewish community followed the traditional way of life. The men worked very hard and, more often then not, so did the women. They were pedlars, craftsmen, small shopkeepers. They tried not to provoke the Christians, but to live in harmony with them. We were all poor, Jews and Christians alike. In the winter the weather was as cold as it is in Montreal."

"And what about Papa?" asked the child.

"Your papa was a craftsman. He knew how to make pottery. Life wasn't easy, and the Jews lived in fear. In the churches, the Christians listened to the priests as they warned their followers to beware of us. They accused us of killing Christ, their God, and never mentioned that Jesus Christ himself was a Jew. Whenever hard times came to the village, the Ukrainians took it out on the Jews. Sometimes violence broke out. They looted and burned our houses and raped the women."

"And Papa? What did he do?"

"Your papa is a gentle man. His character is solid as a rock, but he doesn't know how to raise his hand and strike. He never learned how to fight. He had a cousin, Moishe, who drove the ruffians away, but there were more of them than there were of us, and we had no police or army to protect us."

By now Abe had lost his desire to sleep, and his mother began to sing again. **Yiddish*** lullabies are sad, and the boy loved them. Sometimes, when he had a nightmare, his father, Kalman, would put his hand on his head and bless him.

Kalman always got up early in the morning. He washed his hands as he recited the blessing, thanking God for keeping him alive during the night. Then, like all religious Jews, he wound the **tefillin**, or **phylacteries**, around his arm and his forehead.

* Words in bold face can be found in the glossary, page 107.

Yetta, Abe's mother, explained. "Your papa always put on the *tefillin*, without fail. Even when he was sick, even when he had a fever, he would get up, put on the *tefillin*, and recite the prayer. No one, not even the hazan, the cantor at the synagogue, read the Torah or recited the prayers with a voice as melodious as your father's."

Yetta would make breakfast and then Kalman would leave for the garment factory on St. Lawrence Boulevard, where he worked long hours without complaining.

"Your papa is a brave man. In Ratno, before he met me, he had been married, but his wife took ill and died. I had been married too, and I also lost my husband. Your papa lived on my street and I used to see him coming home from work in the evening, tired and sad. He looked so exhausted that it made me forget about my own troubles. On **Shabbat**, the Sabbath, and on holidays, as we were leaving the synagogue, your papa would speak to me and say something to cheer me up. 'Your husband was a good man,' he would say. Even though he was sad himself, all he thought about was comforting me. Sometimes I would casually wait for him at the door of the synagogue, hoping he would find me. I loved him already, but I didn't dare admit it until the day when one of my aunts secretly told your father's sister that I would be a good wife for him. That was all he was waiting for, he told me later. And so we were married. Not long after that he said to me, 'This is no life for either of us,' and we decided to leave for America. We came to Montreal because your papa had a cousin here, who found us a place to live. Not long after we got here I told your father the great news that God had blessed us. I was going to have a baby – you."

Abe was always asking his mother to tell him about how he came into the world. Every time, the story brought tears to his eyes.

"I was so big that the neighbour women thought I was going to have twins. And they were right."

Here Yetta stopped, and Abe impatiently asked her to tell him the rest of the story, which he already knew.

"When you were inside me, you had a brother, but he left us as soon as he was born. So you see, my darling, you count for two."

She didn't want to linger over the details of his twin brother's death, and that distressed Abe for a long time – until the time when he himself became a father.

The Kleins lived according to the rules of Judaism. They kept a kosher house, which means they followed the dietary rules, never mixing meat and dairy products. They never ate pork or shellfish, and bought their meat and poultry in a kosher butcher shop, making sure that the beef, veal, lamb, or chicken had been slaughtered according to Jewish ritual.

Friday always went by more quickly than the other days of the week. Yetta cleaned the apartment, prepared the Sabbath meals for Friday evening and Saturday, took a bath, and put on her Sabbath clothes. Early in the afternoon, Kalman came home from work, washed, changed his clothes, and left for the synagogue. He always took Abe along with him. With his **yarmulke** on his head, Abe watched the grown-ups stand up and sit down. He listened as the rabbi and the cantor read the prayers. He found it all very boring. His father explained the different parts of the service to him, but he was still impatient to get back home.

When they got home, his mother lit the candles as she said the blessing, and his father celebrated the beginning of the day of rest. He blessed the bread and wine and began singing the *eshet haïl*, the song in praise of the valiant woman, the wife. This was the best meal of the week. As long as he lived, Abe would never forget the fish soup and chicken that his mother cooked.

After the meal his father sang hymns. Abe stayed up longer than usual, and the next morning his father got him out of bed to take him to the synagogue.

The prayers were said in Hebrew. At home, the family spoke Yiddish, and in the street Abe heard other languages, especially French and English.

"Why do we always pray in Hebrew?" he asked his father one day.

The question took his father by surprise. It was almost blasphemous. But he regained his composure and answered in a gentle voice, "We pray in the sacred language, the *loshn hakodash*. It's the language of the Torah, the language of the word of God."

The next day Abe was back with more questions.

"Why don't other people talk the way we do?"

"Other people speak their own language. They aren't Jewish."

"Couldn't Jews speak English or French, then?"

"Of course they could," said his father, somewhat embarrassed.

How could he explain this? He had never thought about it. He said to himself that his son would find out the answer on his own. At the factory he often spoke English. The young owner, who was Jewish himself, looked down on Yiddish, which he spoke very badly. English is the language of the future, he said. Kalman and Yetta had no difficulty expressing themselves in English, but their accent showed their clear and unashamed attachment to their mother tongue. Their neighbours and some members of their community spoke broken English and sometimes French. As pedlars, grocers, or small shopkeepers, they tried to use their customers' language when dealing with them.

It was just before the outbreak of World War I (1914-1918). The boundaries between groups were not well-defined or closed. Sometimes fights broke out in nearby streets between children and teenagers of different languages and religions. In some Catholic churches, priests warned their parishioners to beware of Jews and Protestants. English-speaking Canadians said nothing, but they did not associate with the Jews.

Abe never ventured alone beyond the bounds of his own street. His mother told him over and over again to be careful, but he was torn between curiosity and fear. He was fascinated by other people, but felt threatened by them at the same time.

One evening, when he was four or five years old, he heard his father complaining about the factory owner.

"Do you know what they call our factory?" he asked Yetta. "A sweatshop. It's freezing in the winter and stifling in the summer. We get there first thing in the morning and start slaving away. We aren't allowed to talk because it wastes time. We hardly have time to go to the toilet. It's always occupied and it smells awful. Worst of all, we aren't allowed to be sick. I enjoy working, as you know, but this isn't work, it's slavery. When Mandel Katz complained about it, the owner, Dave, just listened coldly and didn't say a word. On Friday, when Mandel got his pay, the accountant told him that was his last. He was fired. Because he has two small children, he took the first job that came up. It's worse than Dave's plant, he tells us, but I can't imagine how it could be worse."

"But the owner is Jewish," said Yetta pensively.

"That doesn't seem to bother him. Besides, I wonder if he's ever set foot inside a synagogue. And even if he went there every morning, it wouldn't change anything."

Abe often heard his father tell horror stories about Dave, how he used foul language to the women workers and insulted workmen who were as old as his own father.

"Something has to be done," Kalman concluded.

"But what?" asked Yetta. "Perhaps if the rabbi spoke to him..."

"The rabbi? You don't know Dave. He'd listen without saying anything and then keep on doing whatever he pleased."

One evening Kalman brought two men home with him, Mandel Katz and Shlomo Zucker. As soon as they came in, they began patting Abe on the head.

"He has soft, bright eyes," said Mandel.

Turning to Yetta, he added, "I'm telling you, this boy will go far. I can see it in his eyes, and the eyes are never wrong."

Yetta served tea and cookies and gave Abe his dinner in the kitchen.

"I don't know what your father is cooking up with those men," she said, with a worried look.

Two days later the two men were back, and on Tuesday of the following week Kalman did not come home for dinner. Yetta explained to her son that his papa was meeting with friends to join forces against Dave and all the owners like him, who thought of nothing but making money.

As they were leaving the synagogue on Saturday, Abe saw Mandel sidle up to his father. "It's all set," he said. "Next Wednesday, at Joe's restaurant. Everybody will be there."

Abe was frightened. He had the impression that his father was not safe, that some threat was hanging over him, but Kalman soon explained matters to Yetta.

"We're going to form a union, a workers' union. They already have them in New York, and even in Montreal, in other industries."

"Is it dangerous, Papa?" asked Abe.

"Of course not," his father reassured him. "We're going to defend our rights and demand better working conditions and higher pay."

"What if the owners refuse?" asked Yetta.

"Then we'll go on strike, and after that nobody will work for them."

"And who will pay your wages?"

"Our union. We're going to pay dues."

"So on top of all that, you have to pay. It's a disgrace for Jews to join forces against other Jews."

"They're owners and we're workers."

One evening in August 1914, Kalman came home from work with a sombre, worried look on his face. Yetta was alarmed. "It's war," he said, "world war. Great Britain and France have declared war on Germany. Canada will be in it too, because we're part of the British Empire."

"Why is Papa angry?" Abe asked his mother.

"He isn't angry. He's sad and worried. War has broken out, the first war that all countries are involved in. A world war."

Abe sensed that his mother was just as worried as his father was, and wondered whether grown-ups could be afraid too, just like children.

Young Abe was beginning to make out the Hebrew characters in the prayer books and Yiddish newspapers that his father read.

"Soon you'll be going to school," his father told him.

His parents had had long discussions before coming to a decision. Kalman followed the rules of his religion to the letter, even though he had been drawn into secular struggles. Since he was an active trade unionist, and therefore interested in political matters, he kept up with the news about the war that his new country was now involved in. His son would be Jewish, but he would also be entirely Canadian. He would learn Yiddish and Hebrew, but also English and French. It was a rich store of knowledge, but a heavy load for a child to carry.

The French schools did not accept Jewish pupils, only Catholics. This meant that Abe would go to Mount Royal School, which was English and Protestant. After class and on Sundays he would go to the Talmud Torah, or Jewish school. Two sets of lessons side by side.

"You'll take your place as a man in society," his father told him.

Abe enjoyed languages, history, and mathematics.

Every week his father explained to him the *Parashah* of the week, the chapter of the Bible that was read in the synagogue on the Sabbath. Although he was not a scholar, Kalman was familiar with the writings of the Hassidim, those pious Eastern European Jews who were imbued with a deep faith and tried to live out the fundamentals of their religion, not only by studying the sacred texts, but in their daily religious practices. There were teachers among them whose followers remained attached to their writings, stories, legends, and meditations long after the teacher was dead. This was the case, for example, with the most famous of these men, Baal Shem Tov, for whom Kalman had great admiration.

The Hassidim opened the way to mysticism, commonly known as the cabala, whose basic book was the Zohar, or Book of Splendour. Abe was particularly fond of that book, although he was only beginning to understand it.

But when Abe went to the Talmud Torah after school, the rabbi who directed the study of the Torah, the great commentary on the Bible, was not of the same tradition as the Hassidim.

Rabbi Simcha Garber told his students that he belonged to the *Litvack* or Lithuanian tradition, which preached a rational and methodical interpretation of the scriptures, and stayed well away from the emotional and fervent demonstrations of the mystical Hassidim. Torn between these two traditions, Abe decided to follow them both in every respect, to understand and absorb them, so as to be in a position later on to make a choice.

He realized, of course, that the Hassidim were not esoteric, puritan mystics. While they apparently lived apart from society, they were fully integrated into their own community. He never heard Rabbi Garber condemn them. According to them, said the rabbi, only those who love God joyfully can truly serve Him. For them, the holidays are great celebrations. They like to eat, sing, and dance, still strictly observing the precepts of the Jewish religion.

Rationalists like Rabbi Garber seemed to be better integrated into society, more open to other people, but they could be rigid in their reasoning and strict in their behaviour to the point of harshness and puritanism.

Abe had got into the habit of going to Simcha Garber's home after school to discuss his schoolwork as well as the material he was reading. Now approaching adolescence, he took his teacher as a role model, and told his mother one day that he wanted to become a rabbi. His father, even though he believed in his religion and practised it, did not seem very enthusiastic. Religion was all right, he thought, but not suitable as a profession. He was secretly glad when he found on his son's desk a book by Darwin that he had borrowed from the library. If Abe followed the traditional rules, he would not do so blindly, closing his eyes to the outside world, both Jewish and non-Jewish.

ꝏ

From Passover to **Sukkoth**, from *Rosh Hashanah* to **Shavuoth**, the Jewish holidays marked the seasons. *Yom Kippur* is the most solemn day, the Day of Atonement, and comes ten days after the New Year, *Rosh Hashanah*. During the holidays Abe went to synagogue with his father. For *Rosh Hashanah* he liked to hear the call of the **shofar**, not because it was musical, but because it was a distinctive sound, and led up to the solemnity of *Yom Kippur*. On that day even the children were not allowed to speak. On the afternoon of the previous day his father went to the synagogue. As soon as he came back he took a bath. His mother had already taken hers and was busy in the kitchen. Then she dressed for the holiday. When the meal ended, about six o'clock, a period of fasting began, which lasted until sundown on the following day.

Twenty-six hours with nothing to eat or drink. They had to go to synagogue before sunset, when the scrolls of the Torah were brought out. Twelve scrolls, for the twelve historic tribes of Israel. On *Shabbat* only one scroll was taken out of the Ark, unless it was the beginning of a new month, when two were taken out.

"After your **Bar-mitzvah**," his father told him one day, "perhaps you will be given the honour of being one of the twelve scroll bearers."

They had to get there in time to hear the *Kol Nidre*, the prayer marking the year's end, with which the service began.

"But," Abe objected, "we've already celebrated the New Year."

"For ten days," his father explained, "we take stock. What have we done during the year? Do we deserve the forgiveness that we ask God to grant? We ask it for ourselves, of course, but also for the whole community, for all of society. We declare before God that we have sinned, that we have done wrong, even though it was others, known or unknown, who did it."

Before going to the synagogue, Kalman asked his wife's forgiveness for all his angry outbursts, all the unseemly remarks that he might have been guilty of during the year. She also asked his forgiveness. Then the parents, one after the other, in all seriousness, asked Abe, the little boy, to forgive them. Finally it was his turn to ask forgiveness.

In a few months he would turn thirteen, the age of majority in the Jewish religion.

"This year I'll fast too."

"But you're only twelve," objected his mother.

"Twelve years and nine months," he pointed out.

"You'll fast after your Bar-mitzvah," said his father, with a note of uncertainty in his voice.

Abe had the impression that his father was glad to see how eager he was to make his entry into the community.

"Our son is precocious," Kalman said to his wife later.

Yetta was strongly opposed to Abe's wish to fast before he was old enough. Fasting had a strong effect on her. She had periods of nausea and in the early afternoon got headaches that would not go away.

His parents finally reached a compromise. Abe would fast until noon.

"Next year you'll fast like your father."

At the synagogue everyone waited impatiently for the sound of the *shofar*, announcing the end of the fast.

"What I suffer from most is the thirst," said his mother.

Abe's most vivid memory of his Bar-mitzvah would be the moment when he walked up to the *teba*, the lectern in the synagogue. For weeks he studied and repeated the *Parashah*, the chapter from the Torah for that week, which he would have to read before the congregation. On that day, he felt both surrounded and alone. The rabbi was listening to him and the *hazan* was there beside him to help him out if he hesitated and to correct any possible errors.

He would remember especially all those men in the congregation. Their heads were covered and they were wearing the *tallith*, or ritual shawl, around their shoulders. They listened attentively as he read. He had carefully learned the prescribed melody, but this was the first time he had read from a scroll instead of from a book. The words had been written out by hand. He barely looked at them. He had repeated the text so often that he knew it by heart.

"You can never recite the Torah from memory," his father had taught him. "You always have to read the text."

That day it was Abe who transmitted the ancient message to all those men and women. As he spoke it in public, he felt that it was alive. The words were there, written on the parchment for thousands of years, but it was he who was uncovering them and bringing them before the congregation again. It was his decision. He was scrupulously obeying the ancestral rules, but it was his voice that was conveying the message.

He would experience a similar feeling later in life, while reading his poetry in public. At the *teba*, the words belonged to him, even though they were there, written down from all eternity. He alone was master of the words, but he felt very small and very humble compared to the enduring nature of the message.

After the prayers were over, there was a *Kiddush* at the synagogue, a reception during which the rabbi blessed the Creator, the *Shabbat*, the wine and the bread. At home, Abe received many presents of books and clothes.

On the day after *Yom Kippur*, his father set up on the balcony a platform of branches, called a *sukka*, or tabernacle, in memory of the forty years that the Jews spent in tents in the desert, after their escape from Egypt and before they entered the land of Israel. In October, when it was not yet too cold, Abe and his parents put on warm clothes and had breakfast in the *sukka*. More often than not, his father simply read the blessings on the balcony, and they had their meal indoors.

Passover was the most joyful holiday. On the day before, candle in hand, his father would inspect the apartment to make sure there were no pieces of *hametz* bread, or bread baked with yeast, lying around anywhere. For the next eight days they would eat *matzo*, or unleavened bread. From the cupboards his mother brought out the dishes for **Pesach**, or Passover.

His father's inspection had turned up no *hametz* bread. His mother spent days cleaning everything, but sometimes, just for fun, she would leave a piece of this forbidden bread lying in a rather conspicuous corner. Abe would find it and jump with joy at having played such an important part in driving away the enemy.

On Passover evening, the meal was the most ceremonious of the whole year. It commemorated the slavery of the Jews in Egypt and their liberation. A piece of *matzo* was hidden, and the youngest child in the family was supposed to find it. At the age of ten, Abe refused to take part in this game. The words of deliverance and the songs of liberty were beginning to strike a chord in him. He no longer considered himself a child. He was going to be a man and work to free his people from bondage. He would be a worker for emancipation, an artisan of deliverance.

# 2

## *Student, Journalist, Columnist*

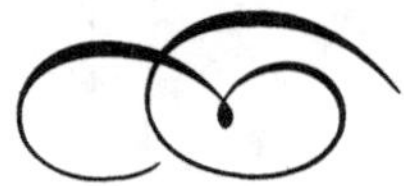

When he was thirteen, Abe entered Baron Byng High School. It was part of the Protestant school system, and classes were taught mainly in English. Many of the students were the children of Jewish immigrants who, when they arrived, had settled in the neighbourhood of St. Lawrence Boulevard. Now they were moving to homes in Outremont, on streets like Querbes, Hutchison, and Bloomfield.

In his new school, Abe had to deal with the contradictions of life in Montreal. Even classes in which most of the students (and sometimes the teacher as well) were Jewish had to start the day with a Christian

National Archives of Canada/C-64042.

A.M. Klein in July, 1926. After he graduated from high school, Abe registered at McGill. From the time he entered university, he was active as a Zionist, a socialist, and a poet.

prayer (although, in theory, the Jewish students were not required to take part).

For Abe, these were years of great discovery. Through the poetry of Milton, Byron, and Shelley, he began to appreciate the beauty of the English language. But he also felt an urge to become familiar with works written in Yiddish and Hebrew, the languages he had heard at home, and he began reading I.L. Peretz, Chaim Bialik, and Sholem Aleichem. He had an irrepressible, almost instinctive, taste for literature, a taste that he was convinced he would never lose.

Abe made other discoveries, too. He discovered friendship and, most important of all, love. It was during this time that he met Bessie Kozlov, shared his enthusiasm with her, and read her his first poems. Some day, he was sure, Bessie would be his wife. These years also saw the beginning of his friendship with another Jewish student, David Lewis, who talked to him about his indignation at the injustice suffered by working people, and the importance of fighting to put an end to poverty.

"We're all children of immigrants," thought Abe. "This is our country and we'll create a different society from the one our parents knew. We have a double commitment, both socially and politically. We Jews know that our future in this world is fraught with uncertainty and danger." As a Canadian, he felt a responsibility for the future of his country. There was diversity there, a separation, but Abe refused to see it as a contradiction. He could be a Jew and a Montrealer at the same time. He could write poetry in English, read the Hebrew Bible diligently, and speak fluent Yiddish and French.

He had already come to believe that human beings, despite their differences and the confrontations and conflicts to which these gave rise, could achieve harmony and experience the richness of their diversity.

Abe's visits to Rabbi Garber stopped, but, as his friend David Lewis would recall later, he continued to observe the Jewish religious laws. He would not travel by streetcar on Saturday, for instance, because it was the Jewish Sabbath, and he would not eat pork, but there were other practices that he may have abandoned, such as the ritual blessings. He had a fear of assimilation, which he saw as a loss of identity. He was quite willing to reach out to others in understanding and friendship, but not at the cost of forgetting his roots and cutting himself off from Judaism and family traditions.

Abe was still in high school when he wrote his first poems, pouring out his concerns and doubts, but always ending with an affirmation of what he was. One of his poems begins:

My father bequeathed me no wide estates;
No keys and ledgers were my heritage;
Only some holy books with **yahrzeit** dates
Writ mournfully upon a blank front page.

He refused to see the world around him as threatening. In his view, anglophones and francophones, Protestants and Catholics, were not his adversaries, still less his enemies. They were simply different, and the only possible course for an honest and upright man, he believed, was to join hands in unity with others, a unity based on the love of God and the need to serve humanity.

Often, however, his faith in others, and especially his confidence in himself and in his own determination, seemed to fail him. He felt vulnerable, subject to weakness and failure. He had lost the unshakable and unquestioning faith that his father and mother had passed on to him. Outside the family home, the world was vast and full of contradictions. Suddenly he found it incomprehensible. The protected child had become an adolescent, a young man. Soon he would be an adult, and would have to fend for himself.

Abe had to make a decision about his future. He no longer wanted to be a rabbi. In 1926, at the age of seventeen, he was in his last year at Baron Byng and about to go on to university. Having graduated from an English school, he naturally chose McGill, where he registered for courses in classics, political science, and economics. To the four languages he already knew – Yiddish, Hebrew, English, and French – would be added another, Latin, which would be a source of pleasure to him throughout his entire life as a writer.

Young Abe found McGill fascinating, but also profoundly disturbing. He had barely left his childhood behind, and now he was thrown into a strange and unknown world. McGill University at that time was an Anglo-Saxon stronghold. Not many of the students were Jewish, and there were even some faculties to which they were not admitted. The university made no secret of its Protestant loyalties. In order to avoid hiring Catholics for the French department, for instance, it recruited Protestant professors in France or Switzerland. Jews entering McGill kept a low profile. As graduates of the Protestant school system, they were of course admitted to that institution, which was a logical next step for them, but they did not always feel at home there, even though the atmosphere was far from conformist and reactionary. There were, in fact, many open-minded students, both Christian and Jewish, looking for comrades in the struggle to remake society and lay the foundation for an autonomous, authentic, and original Canadian literature.

From the time he entered university, Klein was active in three areas, corresponding to his threefold identity as a Jew, a socialist, and a poet.

He became passionately interested in Zionism, which he saw as a living ideal, and asked his father about it.

In the nineteenth century, he was told, Jewish communities in Eastern Europe – Russia, Ukraine, and Poland – were persecuted, and Jews had been looking for a way out ever since. After the pogroms and harassment to which they were subjected, they fled by tens of thousands to seek refuge in western Europe, especially England and France, and in the United States and Canada. But most of them stayed in their own countries and fought to change the social and political situation and thereby eliminate the hatred and persecution that threatened them.

The goal of the **Zionists**, his mother added, was to set up a Jewish national state in the ancestral land of Israel. Everyone who wanted to come would find shelter there, and victims of persecution would be welcomed and protected. Others preached revolution, believing that under a socialist or communist regime anti-Semitism would be eliminated and Jews would have the same rights and duties as other citizens. Some Zionists believed that socialism could go hand in hand with a return to the ancestral land and a rebirth of the Jewish national state. These were the Labour Zionists, who would later play a part in founding the state of Israel.

In 1928 Abe came into contact with a group of McGill students who were both socialists and Zionists, and who called themselves Young Judaea. He joined their movement.

It was in *The Young Judaean*, the organization's paper, that he published his first poems and short stories. His writing depicted Judaism as both contemporary and biblical.

It was at this time, too, that he made his debut as a writer in English. He had absorbed the classics from Chaucer to Byron and Shelley, including, of course, Shakespeare. His verses combined irony and lyricism. He enjoyed the flavour of words, and his poetry often became elliptical or precious, sometimes even degenerating into rhetoric.

On campus Klein carried on the political and social struggle that his father had waged before him. He and his friend David Lewis became leading figures in the McGill Student Debating Society. It was there that he sharpened his skills as a literary critic, political commentator, and thinker.

"A writer has to make a commitment to his people and to society," Lewis kept telling him.

"The only way you can make a commitment is by being true to yourself," was his reply. "A true poet can't be indifferent to injustice and poverty, but the best way for him to act is by being a good poet."

As a socialist, Klein saw no incompatibility, still less a conflict, between his Jewish loyalties and his desire for radical social change. Soon, however, he developed an antagonism towards the communists, which quickly grew into opposition to their theories and activities. He was sharply critical of their stranglehold on culture. In his view, literature could serve society only by remaining faithful to its own values. By putting itself at the service of the state, it lost both its autonomy and its substance. A writer could of course draw inspiration from a cause, and display feelings of revulsion and opposition, provided he expressed himself as a writer. Klein refused to swear unquestioning loyalty to any person, group, or party.

In the late twenties and early thirties Montreal, and especially McGill, were centres of culture, the beating heart of everything that would be important in English Canadian poetry and literature. Renewal was the order of the day. While keeping abreast of what the British avant-garde was writing, the young Montreal writers were also in close contact with the adherents of innovative movements in New York. The centre of interest, however, the first priority, continued to be the still-developing country of Canada.

The Montreal group included both Christians and Jews, united by their love of country and their desire to change its social conditions. Among its members were Frank R. Scott, a poet and law student who would later play a fundamental role in the intellectual and political life of the country; Arthur J.M. Smith, also a poet, who was preparing for a career in teaching; Leo Kennedy, another poet and critic; and Leon Edel, a Jew who would go on to become a professor in New York and the leading specialist on the American novelist Henry James.

During this period also, Klein discovered a young Irish writer named James Joyce. Joyce lived in Trieste and was having difficulty finding a publisher for a novel that was to revolutionize literature: *Ulysses*. Eventually he got it published in English – in Paris. Klein read the novel with excitement and enthusiasm and announced his intention of writing an essay on Joyce.

He became an active member of a group whose slogan, *Preview*, was also the name of its publication. There could not have been a more fitting title. Soon after its arrival on the scene, the group would move into action. It would then reorganize under another name – *First Statement*.

One of Klein's acquaintances was a younger Jewish poet named Irving Layton. He was more detached from family traditions than Klein was, and in talking to his friends he attacked the puritanism that prevailed among Christians and Jews alike. "In my poetry," Layton said, "I will celebrate female beauty and the delights of love, with no moral restrictions."

Klein shared these concerns, but his commitment to the social struggle came first. From 1928 to 1932 he was editor of *The Young Judaean*, the monthly publication of the young Zionists. He also began publishing poems in Canadian and American magazines such as *The Canadian Forum* in Toronto and *Poetry* in New York.

After completing his undergraduate studies, Klein began his studies in law. He had decided some time ago to study in English at McGill and then continue his academic career in French at the University of Montreal. The decision to go into law was not an easy one. He was torn between his passion for writing and his desire to have a family and become an active member of society. He had mixed feelings about political action. Although it appealed to him, he was afraid it would distract him from his plan to be a writer.

He got caught up in politics in spite of himself. In 1929 anti-Jewish Arab uprisings had broken out in Palestine. These events were deeply disturbing to the editor of *The Young Judaean*, and he discussed them with his friends David Lewis and Bessie.

"You should concentrate on studying literature," Bessie advised him.

"Why?"

"So you can write."

"I can write without studying literature. To me, literature is like food and drink. It's my life. I can absorb it without taking courses. The books are there. All I have to do is read them."

Abe was indeed a voracious reader.

David Lewis had told him he had decided to study law, explaining that he needed tools and weapons to defend the underdog. "I can use law as an instrument for changing laws," he said, "but first I have to become familiar with those laws and understand them."

It was clear from the beginning that Lewis had made a political choice. The stock market had crashed in 1929. Unemployment and poverty were widespread. It was a hard, tightly closed universe.

"I have to have a profession," Abe told Bessie, "so I can earn a living."

They were in love and understood each other's thoughts perfectly. Bessie knew they would be married some day.

"Abe is a responsible boy," she told her mother, not daring to admit that they already dreamed of having children.

"He's still young," was the reply.

Bessie's face fell, and her mother added, as if to persuade her to be patient, "He has no profession yet."

Bessie proudly showed her parents Abe's poems that had been published in newspapers and magazines. Her mother smiled and sighed. "He's a bright boy," her father decided.

Abe's parents made no secret of their affection for Bessie. Yetta looked at her son and declared, with mingled pride and nostalgia, "Abe is a man now."

Realizing that he would soon be leaving home, she added, by way of consolation, "Then we'll be grandparents."

"It's all settled," Abe told Bessie. "I'm at law school now, and that means I'll be able to make a living later on as a lawyer."

His friends David Lewis and Frank Scott had already embarked on the same course.

Sometimes he would say, as if trying to justify himself, "Teaching economics at McGill doesn't prevent Stephen Leacock from being a great writer and a wonderful humorist."

"So," Bessie asked nervously, "you'll keep on writing stories?"

"Of course."

Abe was a good student and passed his exams with no difficulty, but his true interests lay elsewhere. He was an avid reader of poetry and continued to read the Bible diligently, but more and more he was beset by doubts. At first they only had to do with religious practices, such as the Jewish dietary laws, which he sometimes failed to observe. He ignored them when he was with his friends, and sometimes with Bessie, but never in an ostentatious or sensational way.

Sometimes it seemed to him that there was a contradiction between what he read in the sacred scriptures and what was required by religious practice. There were days when his doubts grew more persistent, touching the very basic tenets of his belief. For Jews, he had been taught, God is invisible and unnameable. "Jehovah," the name sometimes given to God, is not really a word at all, but a meaningless misreading of a word formed from four letters of the Hebrew alphabet, **YHVH**, representing four words that mean "I am who I am." It is commonly pronounced as *Adonai* (My Lord), or simply *Hachem* (the Name). "What if this invisible and unnameable God does not exist?" Abe asked himself. It was a frightening thought.

Klein's major literary discovery during this period was the philosopher Baruch Spinoza, a seventeenth-century Dutch Jew who had undertaken his own personal reading of the Bible. Spinoza had formulated a philosophy from this reading, and tried, in his writing, to reconcile science, reason, and faith. The Jewish community of that time considered him a heretic and excommunicated him, but Spinoza persisted in calling himself a Jew. His writings did not attack the religion of his forefathers, he said, but were based on free thought and voluntary acceptance.

Klein was in agreement with this line of thought and paid homage to his distant soul brother in a long poem that appeared in the weekly *Canadian Jewish Chronicle*. For Klein, Spinoza was not just an example, but a fellow human being who opened one door for him and closed another, calming his doubts and enabling him to move forward along his own path.

Yes, he said, God exists and is omnipresent. The world is his creation. It breathes the breath of divinity, and every time a misfortune or injustice occurs, the order of divine nature is upset. Every act of cruelty or oppression is an attack on the harmony willed by God and therefore an insult to the Divinity. The duty of believers is to reestablish this harmony, to let justice and equality reign supreme in the world, to serve humanity and human society. In this way, they praise God by deeds as well as by prayers.

Klein found another kindred spirit in the writings of the Jewish philosopher Maimonides. Like Spinoza, Maimonides had been a student of the Bible and had written commentaries on it. He too had suffered persecution and exile. He was born and spent his childhood in Spain in the twelfth century, when it was under Arab rule. Later he moved to Morocco, Egypt, and Palestine. During the Crusades he met the Arab warrior Saladin, who appointed him leader of the Jewish community in Fostat, as the Egyptian capital Cairo was called at that time.

Maimonides was familiar with the Arab Muslim philosophers and was a personal friend of one of the greatest of them, Ibn Rushd, also known as Averroës. He knew the Greek philosophers equally well, and was conversant with Christianity. Armed with all this knowledge, he developed a rational proof of the existence of God and wrote a believer's manifesto.

Klein began writing for *The Canadian Zionist*, published by the Zionist Organization of Canada. He went back to modern sources of Jewish thought. He felt a kinship with Maimonides and Spinoza, who belonged to different centuries and came from widely separate parts of the globe. He wondered whether the issues had not been the same for both of them – how to be true to one's Judaism, to affirm one's loyalty to ancestral and family traditions, while still accepting diversity, the presence of other religions, and the rapid changes that are turning society upside down. Maimonides had tried to create a synthesis of three monotheistic religions – Judaism, Christianity, and Islam – and of Greek thought, in order to affirm what characterizes Judaism and to practise a faith that would be both traditional and contemporary. His *Ani Maamin* (I believe) was an affirmation of faith in God.

Klein wrote regularly for *The Canadian Jewish Chronicle*, a privately owned newspaper with its own printing press, located at the corner of St. Lawrence Boulevard and Duluth Street. It also published the Yiddish newspaper *Kanader Adler* (Canadian Eagle).

He often had lunch with Israel Rabinovitch, the editor-in-chief, who was keenly interested in music and discussed poetry with him. Abe admired the work of Jacob Isaac Segal and translated some of his Yiddish poems into English.

"Who do you want to be," Rabinovitch asked him with a laugh, "Maimonides or Spinoza? One became the leader of his community and the other was exiled."

"Judaism survives outside of institutions," was the answer. "I see no contradiction between those two men."

Another of Klein's friends was Hananiah Caiserman, who worked at the Canadian Jewish Congress. They discussed the direction and orientation of the struggle they were engaged in, and denounced the anti-Semites.

"How can anyone who claims to be a Christian hold anti-Semitic views?" Klein wondered. He wrote strong editorials in *The Canadian Jewish Chronicle*, attacking racial prejudice of any kind.

"Do you see how the politicians operate around here?" exclaimed David Lewis, who already saw himself as a political reformer.

"Somebody has to talk about this, and write about it," Klein replied.

In his editorials, he denounced the corruption of provincial and municipal politicians. He had admired Camillien Houde at the beginning of his career, but years later, when Houde declared his support for Mussolini's fascism, Klein attacked him vigorously. Houde said that French Canadians were fascists at heart, to which Klein retorted that he was twisting words around, that French Canadians were Catholics, which meant that they were motivated by charity and love for their neighbours.

Bessie told him that some of her neighbours had cousins who were trying to come to Canada as refugees but found the doors closed to them. It did no good to tell the Canadian immigration authorities that Naziism was rampant in Germany and that Jews were being driven from their jobs, imprisoned, and sent to die in concentration camps and gas chambers. The stock answer was that Canada was going through the worst economic and social crisis in its history and could not open its doors to foreigners.

It was a human duty, Klein wrote, to give aid and shelter to foreigners trying to escape death. If the humanitarian principles underlying Christianity were ridiculed and ignored, it would mean a return to barbarism.

While Abe was at law school, working as a journalist and writing poetry, the fate of the Jews preyed constantly on his mind, as did the Depression that was ravaging Montreal. Some French Canadians held the Jews responsible for it and accused them of controlling international finance.

"But I have to work to pay my fees," he said to Bessie. "If those people could see my father and his Jewish friends working like dogs to make ends meet, they'd stop talking like that. Who controls international finance anyway? Is it the poor workers and the European refugees who are being turned away by every country in the world?"

"The Jews have to have their own country," he told Caiserman. "The doors of Palestine must be opened to them."

ꝏ

With the bitterly cold winter of 1934 only a memory and the weather once again mild enough for walking, Abe would call for Bessie at her home. Her father was dead now, and her mother worried about her. It was a hard time for everyone.

"Don't stay out too late," she would say to the young lovers.

Alone with her daughter, she would warn her to be careful. "Boys can easily forget themselves, and it's the girl who suddenly finds herself with a big belly."

She was too embarrassed to go on. Her daughter pregnant and unmarried? That would be a disaster.

"You don't know Abe," Bessie protested. "He feels responsible for the whole world – Jews, refugees, working people. So you can imagine, when it comes to the woman he loves..."

But she didn't tell her mother about the plans they were making.

One day in early summer, as they crossed Park Avenue and walked up to Mount Royal Avenue in the shade of the trees, Abe asked her, "How many children shall we have?"

"Wait a minute, dear. We aren't even married yet."

"But you know very well we're going to be married. You're my wife. Till death do us part."

Bessie was touched, and even she herself was surprised by her frank reply. "And you are my husband, my man – for life."

And so it was agreed. As soon as he had passed his bar exam, they would announce the wedding date to their families.

Unlike many of his friends, Klein regularly read *Le Devoir*, *La Presse*, *La Patrie*, and *Le Canada*. He kept abreast of what was going on in the French Canadian part of Montreal, while many of his English Canadian friends felt at home only in Westmount or on Sherbrooke Street West. Neither Jews nor French Canadians could enter their strongholds. The Jews congregated around the synagogues and kosher butcher shops of St. Lawrence Boulevard and St. Urbain Street. They lived on the edge of the French-speaking neighbourhoods on Laurier and St. Joseph Streets. Jean-Talon St. was home to the Italians, Syrians, and Lebanese.

There was keen competition between the Jewish and French Canadian grocers. The Jews closed their shops on Saturday and wanted to stay open on Sunday. In the Catholic churches, the priests preached sermons advising the French Canadians, "Buy from your own people," and urging them not to make the Jewish merchants rich.

"All these barriers must be broken down," Abe exclaimed, and Bessie backed him up enthusiastically.

"Abe believes," she told her mother, "that if the political system guaranteed security for everyone, there would be no more religious conflicts or ethnic fighting,"

"Your friend is an idealist," said her mother. But she could not conceal her admiration and affection for her future son-in-law.

"We should all be able to speak English and French," Bessie went on. "Montreal could become an example of harmony, a centre of understanding."

All around her, her family and friends spoke only English. The young people no longer knew Yiddish and were not learning French.

Then, by way of illustrating what she had said, Bessie added, "Abe is finishing his law course at the University of Montreal."

"I didn't think they let Jews into that university," her mother declared.

"But they accepted him," Bessie exulted.

"Things have changed, then."

"They didn't use to accept Jews at McGill, either. But people catch up with the times eventually. The world is changing, Mama!"

"Do you think so? I hope to God you're right, but I don't see it happening. You're an optimist, just like your father."

Abe told Bessie about his French Canadian friends. They're nationalists," he said. "I can understand them. Jews are nationalists too. We also want to have our own country."

"Why are they against the Jews, then?"

"They're being misinformed. Their priests are preaching anti-Christian principles, often without even knowing it."

In his articles against anti-Semitism, Klein quoted the pope and Catholic intellectuals. Anti-Semites, he declared, had no right to call themselves Christians.

National Archives of Canada/C-64044.

Klein married his high school sweetheart, Bessie Kozlov, in 1935.

National Archives of Canada/C-64034.

Klein (right) with his friend and future law partner, Max Garmaise

# 3

## *Among the French Canadians*

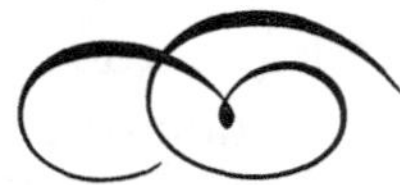

Some of the students Klein associated with at the University of Montreal from 1931 on were nationalists, and he had the distinct impression that the great majority of them belonged to the political right. A few of them had broken with their milieu and were voicing left-wing ideas, but they were careful not to challenge the Church, for fear of endangering their future careers.

Some students were politically active. They came from Liberal or Conservative families – the "Rouges" or the "Bleus" – and were getting ready to enter the fray, following the example of a father or perhaps an uncle.

Abe had joined the CCF (Co-operative Commonwealth Federation), which was like a socialist party and had few French-speaking members. He was saddened and appalled to find that no one around him at the university realized the seriousness of Hitler's recent rise to power. Sometimes people asked him questions about the Jews. Even those who wanted to show their friendship were influenced by the prejudices current at the time. Would he always have to be on the defensive? He was not responsible for the death of Christ and had nothing to do with international finance. He saw that the French Canadians were, on the whole, a kind and generous people, but that they were being deceived by fanatical demagogues and victimized by corrupt politicians. The poems he wrote that year castigated politicians who exploited their people.

He was not prepared to let himself be isolated. Some of the students listened to him.

In a burst of enthusiasm, he said to Bessie, "The French Canadians are just as much my people as the Jews and the English Canadians are."

Abe was interested in French culture and spoke French fluently. To him, the "French fact" was not only a tangible, inescapable reality; it was a source of richness. French was the language of Baudelaire and Victor Hugo, the language of Canada and France, the universal language. He dreamed of finding a way to unite all the different components of the Canadian people.

"Canadians might even invent a language of their own some day," he said to Frank Scott.

Scott, who was interested in French Canadian writers, especially poets, was beginning to translate them into English.

Abe wrote a trilingual poem, combining Yiddish, English, and French, and said to Bessie, "This is our language."

Seeing the sceptical look on her face, he realized that he had let his enthusiasm get the better of him and had tried, without knowing it, to write poetry according to a theory. Nothing could be worse, he said to himself. Theories can kill a poem, and poetry doesn't do justice to the theory the poet is advocating.

His months at the University of Montreal had convinced him that the boundaries between groups were not only artificial, but harmful, and that he, like so many others, had a duty to break them down.

In 1933 he passed his bar exam. He was now a lawyer and could earn a living by practising law. That meant he could marry and raise a family, but this was not the ideal time for such an undertaking. The Great Depression had begun.

"We can't get married until I can earn a decent living," he told Bessie.

"If you ask me, I think you'll always earn enough, but if you want to wait, I'll wait."

What Abe couldn't tell her, and what he couldn't even admit to himself, was that he was first and foremost a writer. True, he was already publishing poems in the Jewish newspapers and in some Canadian and American literary magazines, but that would not enable him to support a wife.

"I'm a man of action," he said, as if trying to console himself and convince himself at the same time.

Bessie knew he was shy and hated crowds. He was afraid of them and only felt comfortable in the company of a few close friends. There he was transformed into a gentle, wonderful, eloquent, affectionate man, who could go on talking forever. She never stopped him, for she knew he would be wounded by the slightest negative word or the smallest annoying gesture on her part. He would fall silent and not open his mouth for hours. Her love for him told her what words and gestures would pacify him and calm him down. His good humour would return and he would be once again her wonderful knight in shining armour.

He often spent the evening at her home, listening to the radio or reading, and Bessie's mother served them fruit juice or soft drinks.

One evening, Abe announced that he and Max Garmaise had decided to open a law office.

Max was a friend and classmate, and the two young men saw eye to eye about the work they would have to do. Max wanted to be a successful lawyer and he knew that Abe, although he took his professional commitment seriously, had other ambitions. He was also a poet.

Max tried to reassure himself. "He's a good lawyer," he said. "He knows his law better than I do."

Perhaps he put too little effort into finding clients, but times were hard for everyone. There was widespread unemployment, more and more firms were going bankrupt, and many clients were lax about paying their bills because they simply did not have the money to pay.

A few months after they opened their office, Abe said to Bessie, "We should set a date for our wedding."

A few months later, in 1935, they were married.

Even though Abe had never gone out with anyone but Bessie, his mother approved of her.

"Bessie will be a good wife," she said.

"Yes," added his father. "When you find the right person, there's no need to look any further."

In any case, Abe had never looked at anyone but Bessie. For him, other women simply didn't exist. For Bessie, Abe had always been the man of her dreams. Day after day, every time she saw him, her feelings were as strong as when they were still going to school.

It was a simple and intimate wedding ceremony, but no less solemn for all that.

When the rabbi asked him to place the ring on Bessie's finger, Abe had the impression that he was seeing her and touching her hand for the very first time. Then came the blessing of the wine, and Abe passed the glass to Bessie. She was so overcome that her hand was trembling slightly. Then Abe was handed a glass wrapped in a napkin, which he had to crush under his foot. In this way, at a time of great joy, Jews are reminded of the destruction of the temple in Jerusalem. For a few minutes, Abe was conscious of feeling the misery of a people struggling for freedom. He felt relieved to think of that at a time when God had sent them such happiness.

"You've known each other for such a long time," Max commented. "You're just making it legal."

That was not quite true, however. From that evening on, Bessie was no longer simply his friend, his companion, his fiancée, his future wife. She was his wife. He was responsible for her life, and they would henceforth share a common destiny. When she had a headache, he felt the pain, and he would be right beside her, taking care of her, anticipating her wishes.

The man of action had now become a journalist. In 1936 he was editor of *The Canadian Zionist*, while still writing for *The Canadian Jewish Chronicle*. He often had long discussions with Bessie about the articles he wrote, and she was the first one to whom he read the various versions of his poems. He watched for the look on her face, and could tell immediately what appealed to her. Her criticisms hurt and distressed him, or lowered his self-confidence. Then, in the warmth of her voice, he discerned her approval or hesitation. For her part, Bessie could read her husband's feelings in his eyes. Often, when he was depressed by his work or by a poem that seemed impossible to finish, his voice would drop. He told her he was just tired, but Bessie understood. She was gentle and told him about little things that had happened during the day. Abe was very grateful to feel her presence, active but not interfering.

For a year Abe devoted himself to his legal work, but kept on publishing his articles and poems. The Spanish Civil War was dividing the western world into two camps. The right wing was supported by the Italian Fascists and German Nazis who were rushing to the aid of the rebel General Franco. The Spanish

Republicans were mobilizing the sympathy and goodwill of leftist movements. Soviet Russia was supporting the Spanish communists and an International Brigade had been formed to go to Spain. Volunteers from all over the world, including Canada, were leaving for the battlefields to lend their support to the Republicans.

Klein was wholeheartedly behind the Republicans. In *The Canadian Jewish Chronicle* he wrote articles about the civil war, which he believed was the prelude to a second world war.

One evening he arrived home in great excitement.

"You know," he said to his wife, "a Canadian military unit is being formed to go and join the ranks of the International Brigade."

"I know. I read it in the *Montreal Star*."

"Don't you think that's wonderful?"

"Yes, of course."

"It's going to be called the Mackenzie-Papineau Battalion. There will be English Canadians, French Canadians, and Jews among the volunteers. We have to fight fascism right from the start, or else it will attack us all, wherever we are."

He stopped. Bessie didn't seem to share his enthusiasm.

"I thought maybe I ought to volunteer."

Torn between surprise and hostility, Bessie stared at him.

"You don't agree?" he asked.

"No, I don't agree," she said in a strong voice, trying to hold back her anger.

"You don't think we have to fight against fascism?"

"Of course I do."

"Well then?"

"Did you think about me? About the child I'm carrying? Who will support us? Even with you here, we have to count every dollar we spend."

She didn't tell him what she was really afraid of. If he didn't come back, how would she survive? Even if she had all the money in the world. War is not a game. People kill and get killed.

Klein didn't bring up the subject again. A few days later, he waited until the meal was over to speak to Bessie.

"That was a wonderful dinner," he began. "Your chicken is just as good as my mother's."

"It was my mother's recipe."

Bessie didn't like Abe's constant references to his mother's cooking when he wanted to compliment her on some dish she had served.

"You know, Bessie, Max and I are finding it hard going in Montreal."

When he was younger, Abe had sometimes dreamed of having a university career, teaching Milton and Shakespeare at McGill, but he knew very well that, being a Jew, he had no chance of being hired as a professor. They would never give his religion or place of origin as a reason, but they would tell him politely that the academic council or some committee or other had had to choose among a number of candidates and unfortunately had not selected him. There would be no point in protesting or making a scene. His friends Frank Scott and Arthur Smith knew that he was perfectly capable of teaching English literature, even though he was not English by birth. Since he had no desire to fight a useless battle, he had chosen law, but he couldn't make ends meet.

"Max thinks we'll get nowhere in Montreal. There are too many lawyers and not enough companies."

Bessie had a vague idea of what her husband was leading up to. She looked up at him without saying anything. She didn't want to leave Montreal. She would be away from her mother, her family, and her friends.

Finally, she said, "I wouldn't really like to go to Toronto."

"Who's talking about Toronto? You know very well that Max and I couldn't practise law in Ontario. We're members of the Quebec Bar."

Bessie took refuge in silence. It was up to him to name the place where he intended to go into exile.

"We're thinking about Rouyn."

To Bessie, that seemed as far away as Russia.

"But," she protested, "we don't know anybody there."

"It's a city where industry is really booming. That's where the future of the province lies. Companies from Toronto and New York are planning to invest there, and there are no English-speaking lawyers."

Had he thought about what their life would be like there?

"I'm thinking of you, Bessie, and our family. We have no savings and times are hard. I have to earn a living."

So he was thinking about her, then, but he was certainly thinking about himself too. Perhaps he was secretly wondering how one could be a Catholic, what it would be like to live as a French Canadian. He was dreaming about how he could identify with other Canadians and still keep on being a Jew. Living among French Canadians in a city where they were in the majority would give him a chance to get to know and understand them.

Bessie knew that Abe was hesitating, struggling. She too had to cope with the Depression. She bought nothing for herself or for the house. Everywhere, people kept saying, "It's the Depression." She consoled herself with the thought that in Rouyn her husband would not be going to those endless meetings of the Canadian Jewish Congress, the Zionist Organization, the CCF, the *Preview* poets' group. He would come home every evening, like a normal husband.

They soon came to a decision. In 1937 Abe left a few weeks ahead of Bessie, found an apartment for them, and came back to arrange for moving their furniture. Then they both left for Rouyn.

People were polite, friendly, and sometimes warm. In the evening and on weekends, though, the Kleins saw no one but the Garmaises. Abe read the papers, listened to the radio, and worked. He had plenty of free time for that. They never had visitors and were never invited to anyone's home.

"Why would you expect them to invite us?" Max asked Bessie. "Who did you ever invite to your home in Montreal? The Chinese? The Italians? The French Canadians and English Canadians?"

"They never invited us either."

"Exactly. You hit the nail on the head. Everyone in their own home. Everyone in their own fortress."

After a few months, the two young lawyers admitted that they were not going to make their fortune in the Abitibi country.

Even though the French Canadians had not taken him into their confidence, Klein had the impression that he had got to know them better in Rouyn than in Montreal. His interest in Christianity, which had formerly been only a rather abstract and distant intellectual curiosity, had now become a reality

The year 1938 promised to be as hard as the preceding year, and the family packed up and went back to their familiar haunts. Bessie's mother and Abe's parents welcomed them with open arms. Abe didn't want to admit openly that the Abitibi expedition had been a failure. Max blamed him for it, even though he realized there was no other solution. The two friends, who had been united in hope and a common business venture, now separated because of something they refused to call by name: failure.

Neither of them was to blame for the failure. Perhaps the venture had been beyond their power. Perhaps circumstances had not been in their favour.

Klein now went into partnership with another of his classmates, Samuel Chait.

National Archives of Canada/C-64037.

Bessie and A.M. Klein with friends.
In 1940 Klein published his first collection of poetry, *Hath Not a Jew*.

# 4

## *Hitler and the War*

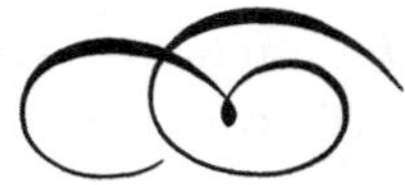

Hitler's screams of anger grew louder and louder during 1938. War was in the air. At Munich the Allies had given in to the German dictator's demand for a part of Czechoslovakia.

"That won't satisfy him," said Abe. "His greed won't stop there. He wants to occupy all of Europe and then become master of the world."

"War is a long way off," said Bessie. "Everyone seems relieved."

"That won't last, and for us Jews it will change nothing. Hitler has sworn undying hatred towards us."

Things were not going well.

"The one thing I learned in Rouyn," said Abe, "is that Canada can't survive unless it recognizes its diversity. In Rouyn, you see, almost all the people were French Canadians, and I felt like a foreigner. Speaking French didn't make any difference. There are other barriers. Religion, for instance, when people don't accept others for what they are, with their religious traditions and practices."

"French Canadians say they feel like foreigners too, in Ottawa and Toronto," said Bessie, "even when they speak English."

Every week Abe wrote an editorial for *The Canadian Jewish Chronicle*. In 1938 the owner of the newspaper, Daniel Wolofsky, who also published the Yiddish daily *Kanader Adler*, offered Klein the position of editor-in-chief of the English-language weekly. His salary would give him only a small supplementary income. He was now the father of a little boy, Colman, and with his legal work he would have to meet the needs of his small family. It was not easy for him to manage, and he was constantly beset with worries, especially since he didn't take on all the cases that were offered to him. He had to be convinced he was defending a just cause, he told Bessie.

She agreed with him, even though she knew that other lawyers were not so scrupulous.

Saul Hayes, the new director of the Canadian Jewish Congress, was also a young lawyer who had studied at McGill. He did not speak Yiddish, but understood it. The secretary of the Congress, Hananiah Caiserman, was more than an ally to Abe; he was a friend who shared the same ideals. Their highest priority, he told Abe, was to save as many Jews as possible.

Persecuted by Hitler, the Jews were fleeing from Germany. After the Anschluss that made Austria a part of the Third Reich, Hitler relentlessly hunted down his political enemies, the communists, socialists, and social democrats. His hatred of the Jews was of a different order. He looked on them as an inferior and malignant race. Young and old, men, women, and children, whether religious or not, and regardless of their political opinions, they all had to be eliminated.

Everyone would have to work together, said Saul Hayes, to bring the Jewish refugees to Canada.

The government in Ottawa was opening the doors to only a tiny number of exiles. The press, especially the French-language newspapers, openly expressed their strong opposition to admitting Jewish refugees. Abe was distressed to read, in *Le Devoir* and *La Patrie*, editorials arguing that there were enough unemployed in the country already, without bringing in more.

Immigrants bring work with them, Klein insisted in his paper. Besides, for Catholics and other Christians, charity ought to have some meaning. During this time, there were Jews trying to go to Palestine, but the British authorities denied them entry, and those who did manage to get there, one way or another, were sent back. A small number succeeded in getting into the country, but most of the Jewish population of Europe would disappear in the concentration camps that Hitler was building.

War broke out in September 1939. Klein had been expecting it, and his first reaction was one of exultation.

"At last!" he exclaimed, "the civilized world is going to stand up to the barbarians who are attacking it."

After the devastating victories of the German armies, his mood changed, first to worry, then to fear. What if Hitler were to win? Klein did not think that was possible, but he was haunted by the nightmare of the end of the Western civilized world, and the total elimination of the Jews, against whom Hitler directed his most deep-seated and fiercest hatred. Then fear gave way to resolution. They would have to fight.

Declared physically unfit for military service, Klein could not enlist in the Canadian army, but he had his own arsenal – the spoken and written word. And at that very time he was contacted by Samuel Bronfman, considered the richest man in the Jewish community of Montreal. Bronfman had decided to take an active part in the life of the community. He had been elected president of the Canadian Jewish Congress and was looking for a man to handle his public relations and write his speeches. He was going to devote his efforts to saving the Jewish refugees and wanted to involve the Jewish community in Canada's war effort.

Klein hesitated at first. Was he, a socialist, a leftist, going to work for this rich capitalist? But, as he said to Caiserman, "We have to use everyone who wants to fight, no matter how rich or poor they are. First of all, we have to defeat the horror and survive. Besides," he added with a laugh, "I'm using Bronfman as much as he's using me. I'm putting my own words, whatever ones I want, into his mouth."

Two important events in Klein's life occurred in 1940: the publication of his first collection of poetry, and his decision to run for Parliament as the CCF candidate in the federal riding of Cartier.

Klein gathered together all his poems that had been published in newspapers and magazines in Canada and the United States. The title he chose, *Hath Not a Jew*, was taken from Shylock's soliloquy in Shakespeare's *The Merchant of Venice*.

For months he tried in vain to find a Canadian publisher for the collection. He realized that in this country there were few publishers for poetry, and the established ones were not interested. He then turned to American publishers and finally had his work accepted by Behrman House Inc., a Jewish publisher in New York. The book appeared with a preface by Ludwig Lewisohn, a Jewish writer who was well known at the time. Klein wanted the collection to show all the dimensions and diversity of his poetry. The influence of the classical English poets, such as Shakespeare and Marlowe, would be seen first, as well as that of contemporary English and American poets like W.H. Auden, T.S. Eliot, and Wallace Stevens. The themes, however, would be those relating to a Montreal Jew inspired by European traditions.

In his book, Klein describes the Jewish festivals and Jewish characters. The influence of Yiddish literature can be seen, as well as that of Hebrew biblical texts and the mystical writings of the Hassidim. Spinoza's ideas also make their appearance.

Klein was convinced that with his poems he had made a notable entry (though not sufficiently striking at the outset) into Canadian and Jewish-American literature. Montreal, especially in its Jewish aspect, was very much a part of it.

While Klein was a Jewish poet, this book was not the work of a religious poet. He referred to Passover, for example, as a festival of liberation and gave a secular meaning to the Jewish celebrations. He tried to depict and establish the independence of Jewish secular life, which, instead of isolating Jewish immigrants from the society they lived in, made them a part of it. He expressed no hostility towards Christianity. Not only did he try to understand Christians, but he urged them to live up to their religious beliefs. He considered it possible to find a synthesis between different beliefs without destroying the identity of each. Everyone continues to be whatever he is, and unites with others, not in religious practice and observance, but in a community of values.

Klein deplored the moral standards of Quebec politics, and criticized politicians who tried to serve their own interests rather than those of the people.

"It's not enough just to criticize," he told Caiserman. "We have to roll up our sleeves and get involved personally. I'm going to run for Parliament."

He chose the party whose ideals were closest to his own, the CCF. Founded in Western Canada, the CCF would come to power in Saskatchewan under T.C. Douglas in 1944, but it had few members in Quebec. The numerically small, embryonic left-wing movement in Montreal also included communists in its ranks. They recruited their members among the educated elite and the trade unionists.

"I'm going to run in Cartier riding," Klein told his friend.

The dominant parties were the Conservatives and especially the Liberals. There were Jews in the riding, but also immigrants of various backgrounds, as well as French Canadians. They all belonged to the lower middle class. Klein had no difficulty in winning the nomination as the CCF candidate. The communists, including the future MP Fred Rose and other Jewish members, attacked him fiercely. The Liberals and Conservatives fought against each other and ignored him or heaped scorn on him.

Klein's shyness made him uncomfortable canvassing from door to door. He gave political speeches before small audiences.

"I haven't the slightest chance of winning," he said to Caiserman.

The other parties began to attack him, spreading slanders about him, and publishing lies accusing him, among other things, of being an agent of a foreign power.

Klein was convinced that he was not cut out for that kind of activity. He was sure he would lose his deposit.

In order to run for office, each candidate had to deposit a sum of money, which would be forfeited if he did not receive a certain percentage of the total vote. Klein had no desire to meet a defeat which would be, for him, more than just a disappointment.

"Why don't you withdraw?" Caiserman suggested.

Bessie gave him her support, but Klein felt nervous all the time, and out of sorts. He did not sleep well and seldom ate a regular meal. She was relieved when her husband told her that he was glad to withdraw, but she knew he would be frustrated for a long time and would accuse himself of lacking courage.

"A person who fights a losing battle may appear heroic," Bessie told him, "but rashness can also be a kind of lack of courage in the face of a reality that you refuse to admit."

For Klein, as well as for his family and close friends, the war years were a very trying time. Worry often deepened into despair. Then, sometimes, very rarely at the beginning, glimmers of hope opened a path to the possibility of deliverance. Hitler had invaded all of Europe and in the space of a few months had become, for the Nazis, master of the world. One country after another had fallen before his armies. First Poland, then Denmark, Norway, Belgium, Holland, and France. The Italians, who had entered the war on the side of Germany, attacked Greece and fought against the British in North Africa.

Klein had been horrified by the announcement of the German-Soviet pact, by which the two most antagonistic countries in Europe divided Poland. A few months later, Soviet forces invaded Finland.

Klein read a large number of Canadian, American, and British newspapers, both Jewish and non-Jewish. He learned that as soon as the Germans entered a country or a city, they put their anti-Jewish laws into effect. Jews were not allowed to hold public office, teach, or manage businesses. They were obliged to wear a prominent yellow star whenever they left their homes. Some of them succeeded in hiding, or finding refuge with Christians, who sheltered them at the risk of their lives, but there were many neighbours, acquaintances, and colleagues who denounced them to the Gestapo, the German police. In some countries, albeit few, there were demonstrations of resistance to the Germans' cruelty. In Holland, for example, the students at the University of Leyden demonstrated against the ban forbidding Professor Meyer to continue teaching law because he was Jewish. In Denmark, the king himself wore a yellow star to show his solidarity with Jewish citizens.

Most of the Jews, however, were arrested by the German authorities, often with the assistance of the local police, as was the case in France.

Bans and harassment of all kinds were followed by police raids. The Jews were rounded up by hundreds and thousands and shipped to concentration camps in Germany (Dachau), Poland (Auschwitz), and Czechoslovakia (Treblinka). From there they were sent to gas chambers and their bodies were burned.

Like all those who followed the news closely, Klein knew the Germans were determined to annihilate the Jews of Europe. He knew that Jews were being arrested and harassed, and that life was becoming impossible for them. But like many others, he was not aware of all the details about the Germans' acts of violence and persecution.

Klein fought in his own way. He was a writer and his weapon was his pen. Not only did he write many articles, but he began composing a long poem, *The Hitleriad*, in which he used irony to denounce the persecution of the Jews. This poem exposed his deep emotion and revealed his inner soul. He felt that it would have some effect and reach thousands of readers.

This poem was published in 1944 by New Directions, a New York publisher. In the same year another publishing house, The Jewish Publication Society of America, published a collection that he called simply *Poems*.

In this book he made use of all the dimensions of his cultural diversity. He translated a poem by Yehuda Halevi, a medieval poet who lived in Spain and wrote in Hebrew. Some poems were patterned after the Psalms. In others, he dealt with contemporary life, attacking, for example, the Padlock Law passed by Premier Duplessis. In others again, he deplored the exploitation of working people and the wretched living conditions of some classes of society. He described the decay of a society that forced women into prostitution. His aim in these poems was to use satire, not to conceal anger, but to give vent to it.

Klein intended *The Hitleriad* to be a poem of action. In it, he denounced the Nazis, exposing their monstrous actions and attacking them with denunciations and satirical terms. He dreamed of reaching the widest possible readership, and even thought that the *Reader's Digest*, the most popular publication of that time, would be interested in publishing extracts from it. The poem combined satire, history, meditation, and journalistic exposé. To Klein's great disappointment, the critics gave it a cool reception. He finally came to the conclusion that the power of the pen was not as great as he had thought, and that a poem, no matter how strong it might be, could not affect the course of history. The great mass of people was insensitive and indifferent to his anger. They were not even aware of it.

Some passages showed the full range of the poet's verbal virtuosity, and it became clear that Klein was a poet of affirmation rather than of denunciation. He had more talent for phrasing lyrics and hymns of glory than for using shock words and calls to action.

National Archives of Canada/C-64043.

The Klein family in the late 1940s.
Left to right: Bessie, Sandor, Sharon, Abe, Colman.

# 5

## *Poet and Author*

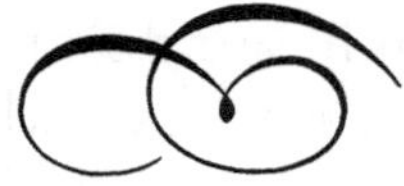

In 1945 the war ended. Klein rejoiced at the victory of the democracies, but for him the struggle was far from over. He was fighting to change the orientation and moral standards of political life in Canada. After long years under the Nazi yoke, Europe was now free, and Canada learned of the crimes committed by the Nazis. Like many others, Klein realized the extent of the disaster, the massacre of the Jewish communities in Europe. The dead were counted. Most of the European Jews had been slaughtered. It was the Holocaust, the **Shoah**.

Klein mourned for the victims and did his best to save the survivors from their desperate plight. Canada's

Jewish community sent help. Services were set up to receive the refugees. The Canadian Jewish Congress arranged for Canadian Jewish families to adopt orphan children who had escaped from the concentration camps.

Klein continued with his writing and worked tirelessly as a journalist. He was disappointed at the reception given to his two books of poetry. Some influential New York critics, Jewish themselves, had not even mentioned the publication of his books. Had they been embarrassed by his Jewishness? Klein wondered. As a rule they spoke about literature in an apparently objective manner which condemned some books to anonymity. Did they ever acknowledge their own identity? Either it didn't exist at all, thought Klein, or else they were making a great effort to conceal it.

Klein wondered whether his openly declared Jewishness was a problem for those critics. If they wanted to comment on his poems, he thought, they could have acknowledged that they were Jewish, or else dissociated themselves from their origin to make a show of neutrality. To avoid such questions and get around the dilemma, they had chosen to ignore it in silence.

In 1945 the dream Klein had nurtured for many years came true when he was appointed a lecturer in the English department at McGill. During the next four years, he devoted himself to his passion for literature. He talked about it; he lived it. And he kept on writing. He had known since his youth that he had no chance of being accepted as a professor of literature at McGill, because he was Jewish And now, notwithstanding his training in law, he was being invited.

Klein taught seventeenth- and eighteenth-century English literature, including Alexander Pope and John Milton. He knew that his own writing at that period showed the influence of those writers, often in a subtle and indirect way. He immersed himself in that literature, while still dealing with legal files at his law office and writing editorials and articles for *The Canadian Jewish Chronicle*.

As a poet, he had chosen to write in English, and therefore English literature was part of his heritage. Because it was his, he read it from the inside, but because he possessed other keys, he also read it from the outside. He mastered Yiddish, Hebrew, and French. He was a Montrealer, a Canadian, a *Québécois* even before that term was coined, but he was of another time and place. He lived in a city and a continent where, although war was present, the scene of battle was far away. Painfully and with great difficulty the Depression had been left behind.

In 1945 and 1946 Canada was rocked by a spy scandal. Igor Gouzenko, a cipher clerk at the Soviet embassy in Ottawa, "chose freedom" and handed over to Canadian authorities secrets about Soviet espionage in Canada and the United States. During those years, Moscow was carrying on intense atomic and political espionage in the western world. Whenever possible, the Soviets recruited communists from those countries, who, because of their faith in and loyalty to communist ideology, handed over state secrets to them.

Gouzenko named names, including Raymond Boyer, a professor at McGill, and, most notably, Fred Rose, the member of Parliament for Cartier. He was the only communist in the House of Commons, and he was Jewish. He was arrested, put on trial, and sentenced to prison for espionage. After his release, the Canadian government allowed him to emigrate to Poland, where he died in 1983,

"We haven't heard the last from the anti-Semites," Klein said to Caiserman. "They'll never stop talking about collusion between Jews and communists."

"The anti-Semites don't need a Fred Rose in order to accuse us," his friend answered. "To them, we're always guilty. They don't let the facts get in their way."

In the United States, after a highly publicized trial, the Rosenbergs were sentenced to death in the electric chair for having passed atomic secrets to the Russians. The couple protested their innocence until the end. The dark years of McCarthyism plunged the United States into a frantic "witch hunt." Senator McCarthy, at the head of his committee, made himself a veritable inquisitor. Leftists, especially intellectuals, were accused of having been active members of the tiny American Communist Party, or simply of having sympathized with its activities.

Klein had no sympathy for the communists, and still less for those who went along with the machinations of the Soviet Union, either unconsciously or in the naive belief that they were serving the cause of suffering humanity.

It seemed clear to him that McCarthy's senatorial investigations in the United States went beyond the bounds of self-protection against foreign espionage. The new inquisitor attacked people whose only crime had been to express opinions that were not shared by the majority.

Firmly opposed to McCarthy's excesses, Klein followed these events closely. He was disappointed that his poems had not reached the masses, and decided to use other ways of finding the millions of readers he dreamed of. He had begun writing *That Walks Like a Man*, a spy novel based on the Gouzenko affair, but it never got past the manuscript stage. Why did he not publish it? Since Gouzenko himself had recently told the story of his adventures in a highly successful memoir, Klein must have felt he could not beat him on his own ground. He decided instead to devote his energy to writing an essay on James Joyce, the great Irish writer who had revolutionized the art of fiction in his novel *Ulysses*. Thoroughly steeped in classical culture, Klein nevertheless was fond of linguistic dexterity and verbal virtuosity, and used it himself in some of his poems. He had the greatest admiration for Joyce's modernism. He saw no contradiction between, on the one hand, a knowledge of the Bible and familiarity with Yiddish literature and English classics and, on the other, the revolutionary work of Joyce, just as he saw no incompatibility between his Jewish identity and his place in Canadian literature.

Once again, encouraged by Lewis and Caiserman, Klein decided to get involved in politics. As a candidate in the 1949 federal election, he ran again under the banner of the CCF.

"This time," he told Caiserman, "I've got to win."

"We'll have to get up early in the morning and roll up our sleeves," was the response. "It isn't going to be an easy campaign."

Caiserman didn't believe he could win, but he didn't want to discourage his friend.

Klein canvassed from door to door and gave many speeches, attracting larger audiences than he had in 1940. He spoke about transforming the world, about the sacrifices made by the peoples of the world in order to defeat Naziism, about the prosperity that was reaching only a small percentage of the population of Canada. He lashed out at the politicians of the traditional parties, the Conservatives and Liberals, denouncing their corruption and lack of concern for the welfare of the underprivileged classes, the absence of positive political programs and social projects. People listened to him, and Klein had the growing impression that he was preaching to the converted and would win support only from those who already agreed with his ideas.

Once again, he bit the dust. His defeat was heartbreaking. Pain and disappointment. Was he not capable of convincing the people he was so eager to serve? How was it possible that these corrupt and dishonest little men, full of ambition but lacking in ideals and scruples, could get themselves elected by huge majorities while he, a man of principle, was rejected?

"That's it," he said to Bessie. "It isn't worth it. I'm not cut out for politics."

She could see that he was depressed. He hardly ever spoke and had lost his appetite. If he played with his children, it was as if he was trying to forget. He was searching for something to occupy his mind.

"You're ahead of your time," she kept telling him. "In politics and poetry both."

"You're just saying that to make me feel better," he sighed.

Bessie protested, but Abe retreated into silence, only emerging to carry out his daily tasks.

He continued to fight, but returned to the only weapon he had left: his pen.

"The English Canadians ignore the French Canadians," he said to Bessie, "often to the point of contempt."

"The French Canadians don't want to hear about other people either," she replied. "They feel threatened by everyone – the English, the Jews, the immigrants. We're the target for their attacks in newspapers and church pulpits."

While living in Rouyn, Klein had become fascinated – haunted, in fact – by French Canadian life. How could he have lived among them all that time without really getting to know them? That had gone on long enough. They won't have anything to do with me? Well, we'll see! It was up to him to take the first step. In doing that, he was only following his deep convictions, giving free rein to his insatiable curiosity and his boundless interest in others.

Klein decided that he would become a poet of his own province, Quebec, even though he was first and foremost a poet who observed its people from the outside. True, he wrote in English and most of the people in his province were French-speaking, but he was convinced that he was doing this as a Quebec writer, totally involved in the life of his fellow citizens. From then on he aimed his arrows at all those politicians and prominent figures who were trying to hold the French Canadians back. He drew realistic portraits: Alexandre Grandmaison, a landowner; M. Delorme, an antique dealer; and others.

Among the French Canadians, Klein presented himself as the poet of all the people. He praised the common people, as he had previously praised those of his own community. The powerful never found favour in his eyes.

He gathered together the poems he had written about Montreal and Quebec in a collection entitled *The Rocking Chair*. It was published by Ryerson Press, in Toronto, the first Canadian publisher to accept his work.

To his great surprise, he received the Governor General's Award for poetry in 1948. Immense joy, intense satisfaction, and pride. He and Bessie took the train to Ottawa to attend the reception given at Rideau Hall to mark the occasion. They stayed at the Château Laurier.

"You've never been so excited," Bessie told him.

Abe felt as if he were walking on air. He was really and truly a poet. His body felt light, and his suitcase seemed to weigh nothing. He was receiving recognition from his country. A committee of Canadian writers had chosen him as the best poet of the year, and there he was, certainly the first Jew, the first son of immigrants, to receive that honour. It showed that his country had really matured as a nation. It recognized all its children, regardless of their origin, and treated them all equally. And what had he done? He had never stopped criticizing his country.

"It's not ingratitude," he said to Bessie, as if he were already speaking to the crowds. "You criticize your country because you love it and fight to make it better. A country's grandeur lies chiefly in the gratitude of those who love it, not only those who praise it."

The publication of *The Rocking Chair* was not the only important event of 1948. In May of that year the state of Israel was founded. Ever since his adolescent years, first as a member of Young Judaea and then as its president, Klein had fought to make that dream come true.

"We Jews have paid an appalling price," he said. "The Holocaust. The destruction of European Jewry. Six million dead. But the dream lives on. It refuses to die."

Klein recovered the religious fervour of his adolescence, but it was no longer simply a matter of religious practices, of prayers and festivals. It was also the realization of the great messianic design. They were rising again from their ashes, to recreate themselves, to build their state and declare to the whole world that they were now a nation. True, they were scattered, and would remain so to a large extent. But for them, however much they were attached to the land of their birth or to their adopted country, be it Canada, the United States, France, Great Britain, there would now be a state they could be proud of and help to build. And there were all the others, the refugees rejected by every country, like derelicts, like unwanted beings. Now they would be welcomed by their own country, a country that would not ask for explanations, but would call on them to roll up their sleeves and set an example, to tell the world that Jews were men and women like anyone else, that they could work on the land or in factories, that they could invent and explore new paths, not only in science and the arts, not only in commerce and industry, but also in agriculture. The country would have its own army, too, so that Jews could fight valiantly and courageously to defend their lives and preserve the peace. No more would they allow themselves to be driven like cattle, with no defence, to the death camps. Never again.

"I'm proud of Israel," Klein declared, "but I'm a Canadian poet. I'm eager to visit the new country, but my own country will always be the one where I was born, where I struggled, where I'll keep on struggling. It's a free country, and I'll fight to keep it that way."

He had suffered discrimination, of course, sometimes in an underhanded way, but things were changing. He was teaching Pope and Milton at McGill, and now, lo and behold, he had been given the Governor General's Award.

# 6

## *Israel, the Great Adventure*

"My one wish," said Klein to Daniel Wolofsky, the owner of *The Canadian Jewish Chronicle*, one day in 1948, "is to go and see, to experience, even if only for a few weeks, the great adventure taking place in Israel."

"You could write articles for our paper," Wolofsky replied. "That would give us a Canadian point of view on the building of the new state. We'll have to find a way to finance your trip."

Klein understood that the paper would pay his salary as usual, but that it was not in a position to underwrite his travelling expenses.

He had two major projects for 1949: to run again in a federal election and – an immensely ambitious

National Archives of Canada/PA-211144.

A street in Safed, Israel (photo taken by Klein).

National Archives of Canada/PA-211143.

A Druze village in Galilee (photo taken by Klein).

In 1949, Klein travelled to Europe, North Africa, and Israel. He wrote articles for *The Canadian Jewish Chronicle* about building the new state of Israel.

undertaking – to write a great novel. The first had ended in a resounding defeat. He spoke about his novel to his wife and his fellow poets. Bessie was enthusiastic and gave him every encouragement.

"Above all," she warned him, "you mustn't worry about having a best-seller. A great work always takes time to find readers."

Klein outlined his project to his friend Frank Scott, who was a poet and lawyer, like himself, and active in the CCF. He was also the son of an Anglican minister. "You want to rewrite the Bible," said Scott. While he appreciated the magnitude of the project, he had doubts about its relevance.

A few days later Klein had lunch with Saul Hayes and Hananiah Caiserman. They told him the Canadian Jewish Congress and the Zionist Organization of Canada were prepared to underwrite his trip to Europe and Israel. The smile returned to Klein's face. Brimming with enthusiasm, he pictured himself already experiencing the fabulous moments that would finally enable him to create the essential work he had in mind.

"I want to see the world as a whole," he said. "I won't be looking for frontiers that keep people apart, but for links to bring them closer together."

Hayes suggested that he stop off in some of the capitals of Europe.

"I won't just stop, I'll visit. I want to see Judaism as an entity, as a living body. We can't help being haunted by the massacre of the European Jews, but that mustn't make us forget, or neglect, our eastern brothers, the Sephardic Jews."

Klein was steeped in Jewish history. He experienced it, not as an isolated phenomenon, or one of minor importance, but as one dimension of the history of humanity. For him, Judaism was not a matter of excluding other religions but of making a choice, a decision. A Jew was a Jew, not because he was ignorant of Christianity and Islam, but because he was fully aware of the facts, because he saw different religions as other options, which he respected and tried to understand.

"Did you know," he asked Bessie, "that the first, the oldest synagogue in Montreal, the Spanish and Portuguese synagogue, is Sephardic?" The Sephardim are the descendants of the Portuguese and Spanish Jews who were expelled from the Iberian Peninsula in the fifteenth century, at the time of the Inquisition. Some of them took refuge in European countries such as France, England, Holland, and Turkey, and prospered there. Benjamin Disraeli, Queen Victoria's prime minister, was a descendant of theirs. And in our own time there is the prominent French statesman, Pierre Mendès-France.

Other Sephardim had taken refuge in the North African countries of Algeria, Tunisia, and Morocco. They had managed to preserve their traditions, but not all of them were well off. The first Jews to arrive in North America were Sephardim who came to the United States from Brazil and to Canada from Great Britain. The French Bourbon kings had forbidden Jews to settle in New France.

Saul Hayes told him that he himself came from a Sephardic background. "But it goes a long way back," he added, with a laugh.

Most Canadian Jews, Klein's parents among them, came from Eastern Europe, to escape the pogroms in Russia, Ukraine, and Poland. They spoke Yiddish.

For Klein, Eastern Sephardic Judaism was part of his heritage. He wanted to get to know Islam and understand how the Jews lived among the Muslims.

As for the Christians, he knew them in Canada. In Rouyn and Montreal he had associated with French Canadian Catholics, and his poet friends Frank Scott and Arthur Smith were English-speaking Protestants.

"I still want to get to the very heart of Christianity," he told Caiserman. "Why are so many Christians anti-Semitic? If they really read the Bible, our Bible and their Gospels, they would at least have some respect for the Jews, even if they didn't love us. I'm going to go to the Vatican and get to know Christianity on its home ground."

In 1949 Klein started out on the grand tour that he had been planning since the previous year, the crucial journey that would produce his masterpiece, *The Second Scroll*.

In Italy he was fascinated by the historic buildings and museums. Each surprise was followed by another, and his admiration for the great artists knew no bounds. He was deeply impressed by Michelangelo's paintings in the Sistine Chapel. He visited the most important sites and sent a report of his findings back to his newspaper.

From there he went on to Casablanca, in Morocco. He found some well-to-do Jews there, of course, but he spent more time in the *mellâh*, the poor Jewish quarter, and was deeply disturbed by what he saw there, an illiterate Jewish community, sunk in poverty, living in a dirty and unsanitary neighbourhood. It made him think of the *shtetls*, the little Jewish settlements in Eastern Europe, where his parents had come from. Had they too, perhaps, lived like that? In Casablanca he went to the synagogue on *shabbat*. The same prayers, the same *Parashah*. The tune was different, but he recognized the words. His far-off brothers were living in a distant era, he thought, centuries behind the times.

He felt overwhelmed. All around these Jews, Muslims were living in the same poverty, the same misery. Why all this suffering? Suddenly, the world seemed closed to him, darkness bore down from all sides. In Europe the Jews were being massacred and anti-Semitism was raging, despite Christ's message of love. And there, in North Africa, his brothers, only dimly aware of their dignity, were wallowing in ignorance. Did he have the right to impose on them his point of view as a privileged North American? Was he insensitive to their fate? If he could speak to them freely, if he could find a common language, he would hold out his hand and communicate his feelings to them, let them know that he was their brother. But what was the use? He would not understand them any more than they would understand him.

He would write. He would tell of his anguish in the face of a world where, on all sides, humanity's honour was trampled underfoot, its dignity crushed, and its right to well-being ignored.

On August 2, 1949, Klein landed at Lod Airport, near Tel Aviv. It was a moving experience for him. Dark thoughts and haunting fears were left far behind. There he was, present at the rebirth of his people, their return to life. His articles waxed lyrical. Here was a whole people rising out of its ruins, resurfacing in the world, pitting its determination and courage against hatred. Ashkenazis and Sephardim, eastern and western Jews, men and women speaking a multitude of languages, carrying in their memories a burden of pain and suffering – they were all there together. Now they were learning a common language, a language both old and new – Hebrew – and reconnecting with themselves, with the strongest and noblest part of themselves.

Here were men and women opposing the world's hatred with a will to live, to be happy, to be at home on their own soil, in their own rediscovered and reviving land.

While he was there, Klein witnessed the return of the body of Theodor Herzl, the founding father, who had been the first to do more than just dream. He had thought and planned and given birth to the Jewish state. Like Klein, he had been a journalist and a man of action, and now his remains were returning to the country he had built out of his dreams and especially by his determination.

It seemed to Klein that history was unfolding before his eyes. He was experiencing its events one after the other. At the beginning of the century Herzl, then the Paris correspondent for a Viennese daily, had covered the trial of Alfred Dreyfus, a Jewish officer who had been falsely accused and convicted of treason. The humiliation of this French Jew had affected not only his family, but his entire community. But French justice and honour had been defended by courageous men, both Jews and Gentiles. Émile Zola had shouted "I accuse" and demanded a new trial. France had been split into two camps: pro-Dreyfus and anti-Dreyfus. Finally, the man's innocence had been acknowledged and proclaimed.

Herzl had witnessed these events and come to the conclusion that Jews could never find happiness until they had a state of their own.

The return of Herzl's remains to the planned and rebuilt country was an essential act of memory. The founder was being recognized by his people, who had been scattered throughout the world and finally reunited. They built a cenotaph to the man who had transformed hope into expectation and expectation into reality. Klein wrote a moving account of the ceremony.

In other articles, he described the state of Israel as it struggled with its many problems. First was that of security, since its existence was threatened by its Arab neighbours. Another weighty problem was that of taking in refugees, the survivors of the death camps. Then, too, there were all the Jews from the Arab countries who were beginning to flock in. The first priority was to provide housing for them all. They were placed in tents, wooden shacks, temporary camps. They also had to be rehabilitated physically and especially mentally. They had to be taught the language.

It was a moving experience for Klein, who read Biblical Hebrew, translated it, savoured it, absorbed it, to hear it spoken as the language of the street. Here was a language that had been preserved through the written word, through the sacred texts, through prayer, and was now, centuries later, becoming the language of everyday life. How else could these scattered multitudes, speaking so many dialects, be united, except by giving them a common and unique language? It was a language they had never forgotten, because, through all the centuries, they had reserved it for prayer, for praising the Lord, and for repeating their hopes and expectations.

Through his efforts to take part in their life, Klein became aware of the scattered and diverse fragments of his people. There they were, reunited on their ancestral land.

And what about the others, those who still lived in the countries of their birth, who were working in the countries they called their own? They were not all going to pack up and leave for Israel! The horror had had to fall on the Jews of Europe, a continent to which they had contributed so much in the intellectual, artistic, scientific, and industrial fields. Now some Arab countries were mistreating and harassing them and making life difficult for them. They were emigrating en masse from Yemen, Iraq, Egypt, Morocco, and Tunisia. And yet, despite their painful recent history, some Jews still remained in Europe.

What could be said about the Jews who were living comfortably in their own countries? Those in the United States, Canada, Brazil, Argentina? They greeted the birth of the new state with all the emotional strength at their command. They were proud of it. But they had no intention of going there to live.

One day, as Klein was pouring out all his fervour and emotion to an Israeli journalist, the latter, surprised and critical, asked him, "What are you waiting for? Why don't you lend a hand yourself? We need all the help we can get. Admiration is very nice, but it doesn't put food on the table. Emotion without action is useless."

Klein was taken aback. "You're right," he said.

How could he explain his choice to this man who had already made his own decision, who was not content merely to record the birth of the new state, but who was helping to build it? How could he tell him that his community was in Montreal, that his country was Canada?

In his articles, Klein addressed the Israelis in a fraternal way. Don't blame those among us who don't come to join you, he said. They are with you in their hearts, but the country of their birth will always be their only country as long as they can live there on a basis of equality with other citizens, and still remain distinct. Our distinction is not one of superiority, and confers no privileges. It is our particular way of being part of the human community, of taking part in its advances and its progress.

In other articles, Klein asked Canadian Jews to understand why the Israelis were so impatient to see other Jews come and join them, to take part in their struggle and share their life. There might be a note of arrogance in their call. The beginnings of the state were all the more heroic since they involved a moral and spiritual rehabilitation, a yearning for reconciliation and peace.

It was important to reestablish dialogue with other countries and nations, on a new basis of equal exchange. Was not he himself, Abraham M. Klein, an eloquent example of the possibility of such dialogue? Although he had been a militant Zionist since his youth, he considered himself first and foremost a Canadian. His province was Quebec and his city was Montreal. That was where he had lived and where he intended to go on living.

One of the objectives of his journey was to get to know Christianity and Islam. Not only to understand how Jews fitted into the civilizations that had grown out of those religions and how the Christian and Muslim countries treated them. That was part of it, of course, but what Klein wanted to know was how Christians and Muslims established their relationship with God. These religions had been born out of Judaism. Was it possible at last that the three monotheistic religions might affirm their basic community, put an end to fratricidal wars, and bring about peace on earth? He also wanted to see how artists belonging to those religions raised monuments, praised and celebrated the Creator, and whether, in their diversity, they could join their voices and talents in a common act of praise.

National Archives of Canada/C-58349.

A.M. Klein's masterpiece, *The Second Scroll*, was published in 1951. Here, he presents a copy of the book to a representative of the Canadian Jewish Congress.

# 7

## *The Second Scroll*

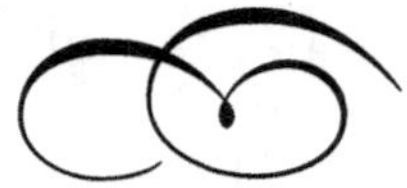

The articles Klein sent to *The Canadian Jewish Chronicle* were only preliminary steps leading to the great work that he was developing and would eventually write. As soon as he was back in Canada, he set to work on his masterpiece, *The Second Scroll.*

When the book was published in 1951 by Alfred A. Knopf in New York, it met a lukewarm reception. It was some time before its importance was recognized. It fell like a pebble into a pond. It belonged to no particular category and followed no particular style. It defied classification. Was it biblical exegesis? Yes, but it included too many metaphors, too many images, too many symbols. Was it the writing of a visionary? Yes, but it contained precise facts, referred to historical events and well-known places. Was it the work of a poet? Yes, but it was too realistic, too closely patterned after the biblical text. It was all those things at once.

Klein was not only a diligent reader of the Bible and of classical Hebrew literature. He was also steeped in classical and modern English literature, from Milton to Joyce. He was a visionary with an unbridled imagination, but he was also a journalist who reported facts as he saw them, and nothing more.

It took time to gauge all the dimensions of this work. In his explication, Klein made use of resources from various cultures, from all his knowledge, observations, and life experiences. It was a summing up and a balance sheet. But above all, it was a work of literature, in which poetry, meditation, knowledge, and life combined to produce a result that was both complex and simple, original, but not at all foreign or unusual.

Years went by before there was any recognition of Klein's unique and essential place in English Canadian literature and, through it, in the literature of the world. *The Second Scroll* was not published in French until after Klein's death, when Robert Melançon, a Quebec poet, also from Montreal, who loved the work and recognized himself in it, translated it carefully and affectionately, with the help of his wife Charlotte.

The book can be read at several levels. First of all, it is a story, with incidents, sudden developments, ups and downs, and *coups de théâtre*. It is also a symbolic work, in which Klein retraces and summarizes the history of humanity and its struggle for emancipation, as well as the struggle of the Jews down through the ages.

To do this, he borrowed the form of the Bible, reproducing its chapters and episodes. Then again, *The Second Scroll* is a work of poetry, in which man is involved in a battle between the forces of good and evil. After he is saved, he awaits the coming of the messianic age, when all religions will be joined in a common response to the divine call, in a universal cosmogony in which art and science will unite and guide humanity towards its accomplishment

*God of Abraham, God of Isaac, God of Jacob, who hast bound to the patriarchs their posterity and hast made Thyself manifest in the longings of men and hast condescended to bestow upon history a shadow of the shadows of Thy radiance;*

*Our prayers accept, but judge us not through our prayers: grant them with mercy.*

*Make us of Thy love a sanctuary, an altar where the heart may cease from fear, and evil a burnt offering is consumed away, and good, like the fine dust of spices, an adulation of incense, rises up.*

*Oh, accept, accept, accept our thanks for the day's three miracles, of dusk, of dawn, of noon, and of the years which with Thy presence are made felicitous.*

*Grant us – our last petition – peace, Thine especial blessing, which is of Thy grace and of the shining and turning of Thy face.*

In the book, the story begins at the beginning, that is, following the sequence of the biblical text, with Genesis. The narrator, a Jewish writer from Montreal, learns about the vicissitudes of life from his uncle,

Melech Davidson, a pious Hassidic Jew, who has thrown himself into a political struggle on the side of the left.

*Melech* is the Hebrew word for "king." By his name, this character makes reference to King David, or rather to his descendant. It is at the same time a reference to the Messiah, who was to be a descendant of King David. The forces of evil are represented by those who incite pogroms (the same ones who drove Klein's parents out of their native Ukraine at the beginning of the century), as well as by the Hitlerite and Stalinist police.

The narrator is a child who comes to awareness through the stories his parents whisper to him about his fabulous uncle. Catastrophe strikes Ratno, the native town of the narrator's parents. Two survivors arrive with the news that Melech is still alive.

In Exodus, the second chapter, the narrator, now grown to manhood, is a journalist in Montreal. The editor of his paper sends him to do a report on the newborn state of Israel. By a surprising coincidence, a letter from a refugee camp in Bari, Italy, is delivered to him; it is from his uncle. Melech describes in his letter the fate of the Jews in Europe. Having repudiated Marxism, he returns to Judaism, and, while he does not become an orthodox Jew, he takes up the traditional religious practices.

In chapter three – Leviticus – the Montreal journalist goes to Bari, but arrives too late. He is told that his uncle has gone to Rome, to the home of a friend, Monsignor Piersanti. When the journalist gets to Rome, the Monsignor tells him that his uncle is no longer there, and describes him as a man in search of God, a man who, in his discussions with Piersanti, explored the Christian dimension of human civilization. The narrator, carrying his uncle's letter in his pocket, is attacked in the street by a band of ruffians led by a certain Settano, whom he had met the evening before in a hotel. Settano suspects him of carrying a secret message.

The narrator escapes from the band and visits the Sistine Chapel. In his description of this visit, Klein launches into a personal analysis of the work of Michelangelo, seeing in it the fate of humanity. Both Jews and Christians are present. He perceives there the existence of a united humanity, reconciled in its longing to rise up toward God.

In chapter four, which corresponds to the book of Numbers, the narrator reports that his uncle, on the way to the land of his forefathers, did not feel ready to go there without stopping off in Morocco to meet his Sephardic brothers, without whom the Promised Land could not become the Rediscovered Land.

In Casablanca Melech observes the degradation of his brethren. To express his revulsion and refusal to accept the situation, he organizes a demonstration of beggars. Arrested by the Muslim authorities, he is released through the intervention of an American Jewish organization, and goes on to Israel. He is not abandoning his Sephardic brethren, but concludes that they will never achieve freedom except by their own efforts. Before they can recover their dignity, they will have to rediscover their own resources.

The following chapter, Deuteronomy, finds the narrator in the land of Israel, exploring its religious aspects. In the town of Safed he immerses himself in the cabalistic, mystical branch of Judaism. The book ends with a repetition of the morning prayer and with a psalm. (In his translation, Robert Melançon preserves the ancient language of the psalm by using Old French.)

*I will extol thee, O Lord; for thou hast lifted me up, and hast not made my foes to rejoice over me.*

. . . . . . . . . .

*Shall the dust praise thee? Shall it declare thy truth?*

*Hear, O Lord, and have mercy upon me: Lord, be thou my helper.*

*Thou hast turned for me my mourning into dancing: thou hast put off my sackcloth, and girded me with gladness;*

*To the end that my glory may sing praise to thee, and not be silent. O Lord my God, I will give thanks unto thee for ever.*

In *The Second Scroll*, Klein's intention was to represent the Book. An introduction to the Bible, a return. Klein relives, in the present, its various episodes. In this way, time is abolished, and through the poet's voice, through his reading, the Bible appears as a contemporary book. *The Second Scroll* is also Klein's personal story. It contains many autobiographical elements, which blend into the fate of a people and are transformed into episodes, or fragments, of the fate of the Jews.

ෙ

While his major work was slowly making a name for itself, Klein become more and more overcome by worry. He was plagued by doubt. He believed that *The Second Scroll* had reconciled him with Judaism, just as he had tried to reconcile Judaism with other religions – Christianity and Islam. He could finally be free in his beliefs, in harmony with himself, his traditions, and the world.

But for several weeks he had been sleeping badly, waking up suddenly, plagued by nightmares.

"I may have committed the worst of all sins," he said to Bessie one evening,

"What sin?" she asked.

"A Jew can only write commentaries on the holy word, and articles in praise of it."

"That's all you've done," said his wife, reassuringly.

He was not as firmly convinced of that as she was.

"But calling my book *The Second Scroll*, following the biblical text, one episode after another..."

"That was just a way of saying that the Bible is a living book, read by a man of the present time, a book that immerses us in the present, explains the world to us, provides a context for the events that we experience."

Bessie was becoming excited. She felt the greatness of the book, and she knew what it had cost her husband to complete it. Hours of fever, sleepless nights, headaches. She had done her best to protect him, urging her children not to make a noise, to let their father work.

National Archives of Canada/C-83740.

Bessie and A.M. Klein in 1955. Bessie was always at Abe's side. She never complained, and she was always there to take care of him.

# 8

## *The Great Silence*

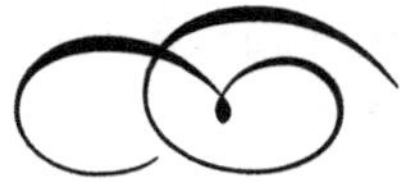

As soon as Klein returned from his travels, the Canadian Jewish Congress organized a cross-Canada speaking tour for him. This was followed by many invitations. With the emotion of a poet, a Jew, a man thirsting after liberty, he spoke about the rebirth and building of Israel in simple and well-chosen words. He described the difficulties and harsh life of the builders, but also spoke of their courage and heroism. He did not rouse crowds with slogans, but shared his feelings, fears, and hope with individual persons.

Wherever he went, from Toronto to Winnipeg, from Regina to Vancouver, he found Jews like himself, who listened to him, hanging on his every word, with tears in their eyes.

Klein slept badly, and spent long evenings in discussion with the people he met. He ate badly too, either too much or not enough. At night, alone in his hotel room, he was tormented by doubts. Between tours he would return to Montreal, exhausted, and spend hours resting. Then he would suddenly get up and rush to finish an article or an editorial that his paper was waiting to send to the printer.

The Canadian tour was followed by an even more strenuous American tour. From New York to Chicago, from Philadelphia to Los Angeles, Klein encountered the same kind of audience, the same faces turned towards him, their attentive eyes shining with emotion and enthusiasm.

For days on end the poet gave way to the eye-witness. Neither a spokesman nor a propagandist, he defended no cause and had no agenda to carry out. A man among men, he had seen and experienced what all these women and men were reliving through his words. The power of the word, which disappears as soon as it is spoken, but leaves traces engraved on hearts and memories.

The poet was still there, in the background. His words had to be heard from a certain distance. He had already said everything in *The Second Scroll*. But Klein kept asking himself, "Have I really said everything?" There is no definitive book, no final text, only attempts and approximations.

The papers reported alarming news. Israel's neighbours refused to accept the existence of the new state. Anti-Semitism was still to be found in other parts of the world, including Poland, where there were hardly any Jews left, after three million of them had been murdered and burned in the Nazi crematories.

What good were words? And what about all the books written since the dawn of time, and all the great thinkers from Socrates to Spinoza? They had already said all there was to say, but had they been able to convince anyone but themselves? The sacred text, all the appeals for love and brotherhood, were being turned upside down, changed into instruments of persecution, oppression, and murder.

And so Klein kept on making speeches, and late at night, alone in a hotel room, tossing and turning on his bed, trying in vain to fall asleep, he kept asking himself, "What's the use?"

Tired and worn out, he felt impoverished and powerless. He had devoted his life to others, so that the world might be more accepting of the poor and forgotten, so that their lives might be easier. And now he himself felt like the poorest of the poor, because he possessed nothing but words, and they were becoming devalued and useless.

One morning, after another restless night, Klein woke up in a particularly feverish state and began pacing the floor. Bessie woke up and, not finding him in bed beside her, leaped to her feet.

"What are you doing?"

"I can't sleep. I'm never going to be able to get to sleep again."

He was panting and his face was lined with fatigue.

"When are you going to stop carrying all the world's burdens on your shoulders?"

"What's the use of it all?"

"What do you mean, 'all'? Your wife? Your children?"

"Do we have the right to bring children into the world? What kind of life are they going to have?"

"Don't worry about that. Your children will grow up. They'll cope. They'll make their own world, just as we made ours."

She made coffee and toast.

"Here, eat a little something."

"I'm not hungry, I've lost my appetite."

"You have to eat all the same."

Klein was too exhausted to move. Bessie forced some toast into his mouth. Robot-like, he made no resistance.

"Aren't you going to the paper today?"

"For what?"

Bessie sighed. The children were now up and getting ready for school.

"Isn't Papa well?" asked the eldest.

"Oh yes, he's fine."

"What's wrong with Papa?" asked the other.

"Nothing. He's just a little tired. He's working too hard."

Bessie led Klein back to bed and phoned the paper to tell them he was ill.

The next day, Bessie went along with him to the paper.

"He hasn't been the same for some time now," said Wolofsky. "He's gloomy, morose, irritable."

"He's tired. He's working too hard, and all this travelling is wearing him out."

"But travelling is the only thing he wants to do. That's all he asks."

"It's as if he were running away," she said, partly to herself, "running away from himself."

In the afternoon Klein came home, half asleep. Bessie left to do some shopping. When she came back she found him shaved and dressed, ready to go out.

It was an autumn day. The air was brisk and there was a piercing north wind, a reminder that winter was knocking at the door.

"Let's go for a walk on the mountain," Bessie suggested. "The way we used to do when you wrote love poems for me."

"Writing poems! That was so long ago! What a useless waste of time! You have to be really naive to base your life on that."

"Abe, you're a well-known writer. People admire you."

"What people?"

"Everyone who matters. Everyone who understands you."

"But there are so few of them!"

Klein reluctantly dragged himself after her, but soon he was out of breath and exhausted. Bessie suggested they go home.

"I failed. Another failure. I can't even go for a walk with you."

Bessie made some sandwiches, while Abe listened absent-mindedly to the radio, a newspaper in his hand. He ate like an automaton. With his vacant stare, he looked like a broken man, going resignedly to meet defeat.

In the evening he sat down at the table and had dinner with the children. He answered their questions in monosyllables.

"Let your father rest," Bessie said finally.

"Rest? He didn't even go to the office. Why is he tired?"

"I'm tired of life," said Klein in a low voice.

Stunned and worried, the children turned questioning looks towards their mother. Bessie felt confused and irritated. She said to her husband, "Abe, don't talk such nonsense."

That morning, she had asked the pharmacist for some sleeping pills. Before going to bed, she handed one to Abe, and he swallowed it without question. Haggard, without washing, he lay down on the bed and fell into a lethargic sleep. Bessie lay down beside him. He slept very restlessly. At daybreak, she realized that Abe was not in the bedroom. Frightened, she rushed out into the living room, where she found her husband lying motionless on the floor, a vacant look on his face.

"Abe, Abe," she shouted. There was no answer.

She shook him. He made no resistance, but lay there, glassy-eyed, without saying a word. She called the hospital and, an hour later, he was taken to the emergency ward. He had swallowed a whole vial of sleeping pills, and the doctor decided to keep him there for a few days.

When he came home from the hospital, Abe seemed to have regained his energy. He went to work, wrote articles, and answered his mail.

A few days later, Bessie found him, early in the morning, slumped in an armchair in the living room. She called the doctor, who prescribed a sedative.

Two days later, Abe got up as usual in the morning, joked with his children, and went off to work.

When he came home he was cheerful and bubbling over.

"I want to make another tour," he announced.

"No," said Bessie. "You can't. You need to rest."

"I'm not tired."

"Yes you are, even if you don't admit it. You're asking too much of your body."

"My body is not the problem."

He put his hand on his forehead.

"That's where the problem is, in my head. That's where I'm not right."

The doctor had told Bessie that Abe was going through a critical period. He was suffering from depression. No one could say how long this illness would last.

"Tomorrow you're supposed to take part in a round table discussion at the Jewish Library," said Bessie. "David Rome called to confirm it."

"All right."

The next day, at seven in the evening, Abe was stretched out in his armchair, motionless.

"It's time," said Bessie. "You'd better get ready."

"Time for what?"

"You know, for the meeting at the Jewish Library."

"I've got nothing to say."

"But you agreed to take part in the round table discussion. That was weeks ago. They've put announcements in the papers and sent out invitations. You have to go."

"I've got nothing more to say."

"You can't do this, Abe. You have to go."

"I have nothing to say. Anyway, my words would fall on deaf ears, as usual. I've spent my life talking, shouting, writing. It's no use. All in vain. An absolute waste of time. That's enough. I've done my bit. I've got nothing more to say. Did I ever have anything to say, anyway? People might have listened to me, heard me. But no. No one is interested in my rambling, in my wild imaginings. No one was ever interested in it."

A little later the phone rang.

"Don't answer," said Abe. "They can get along without me. The others will speak. There are always people with nothing to say who get up to speak."

Several times during the evening, the phone rang, but Bessie didn't move. The doctor had warned her. The effects of depression are unpredictable. All she could do was arm herself with patience and wait for it to pass over.

The journeys that he had so longed for had become a burden. From being a source of support which he had counted on for deliverance, even briefly, they had become ordeals that he no longer had the strength to cope with.

Wolofsky called to ask him for articles, but he couldn't manage to finish them on time. At the last minute, Wolofsky had no choice but to replace them with articles reprinted from American Jewish newspapers. That was not a solution.

The doctor had prescribed some pills, and since then Abe had been sleeping well – too well. It was all he could do to drag his inert mass out of bed, and when he did get up he would sit for hours, numb and vacant.

It became harder and harder for Bessie to conceal her feeling of helplessness, which, as the days and weeks went by, was turning into despair. When she tried to speak to her husband he answered in monosyllables and always agreed with her. At the beginning, he had sometimes raised his voice slightly. "You can see very well the state the world is in," he would say. And he would end with "What's the use, then? You can see very well that everything we do, all our talking, is useless!"

Bessie saw that her husband's absent-mindedness and silence could not be explained only by his illness. He was losing interest in the outside world. Life was becoming mechanical and empty. He could have left everything and gone to live a solitary, ascetic life in a far-off desert. But he loved his wife and children too much to abandon them. Perhaps he thought that a presence, even if minimal, was still a presence. Bessie never complained. She was always there to take care of him.

In spite of everything, Klein continued to write articles. When he took them to the paper, he would say, with a sad smile, "Who's going to read that?" Wolofsky thought he could reassure him by quoting the number of subscribers and mentioning letters from readers. "Oh, yes!" he would exclaim, "sometimes you might find a reader. What difference does that make? Even the ones who write letters! How many of them are prepared to go further, and take another step?"

In his calmer moments he said, as if trying to convince himself, that reading had transformed his life. Yes, but he was talking about the Bible, Spinoza, James Joyce. What about himself? He was far from being included in that company. He had not reached such heights.

One morning, Klein got up early, put the *tefillin* around his forehead and his arm, recited the prayer, and collapsed in tears. What right did he have to write? Had he read the sacred text enough to speak about it? If not, it was blasphemy, it was a sin. He was only a poor man who had to go on reading and rereading the Text. Later, perhaps, he could speak out, voice an opinion.

What pride, what vanity, had prompted him to write? His blindness had been so complete that he had wanted to imitate the Bible, even to rewrite it. He tried to calm himself by saying, "But that was only the commentary of a humble reader."

Did he still believe in these texts, which his father and his teachers had taught him? What did it matter? He had never gone through the door of the enclosure, the door that connected him to his community, to his people, and, through them, to all humanity.

"I only offered homage, I was only a celebrant," he said, defending himself before an invisible accuser.

So many hopes dashed, so many vain expectations, so many promises not kept!

And now some survivors of the concentration camps were going home to Poland. What was waiting for them there? A warm welcome? Joyful reunions? Nothing of the sort. Another pogrom, a new one! Yes, there were men and women who wanted nothing to do with the survivors, who wanted to get rid of those who were left. A few hundred. A few thousand at the most. Three million Polish Jews had been killed, and there was still no room for these castaways!

Oh yes, there was a courageous act here and there, a generous gesture, but they were drowned in an ocean of hostility and hatred.

When words are powerless, he thought, there is a great temptation to give way to violence, which turns first against the perpetrator. He knew that. The first victim of an act of violence is the one who commits it. He resigns. He defiles what is most noble in him – his humanity. Klein knew that he himself was incapable of that. His fits of anger, usually directed against himself, became attempts at understanding and finally turned to pity and compassion.

Does a Jewish writer sin against Creation by pretending to be a creator? The writer's endeavour, the words, sentences, and pages wrenched out of his meditation and reflection, out of his joy and suffering – was it all vain and pointless? Are words powerless, and therefore superfluous in the face of violence?

Abe would sit for hours on his balcony. The telephone would ring, but he would not hear it. The children would go out and come in, but he would not see them. Bessie would bring him food and he would eat it mechanically. He was simply not there, either in the world or within himself. Neighbours passing by would look at him, and after a while they would not even see him.

One day some children were playing ball in the street. A car drove by and one of the children, chasing the ball without looking, nearly got run over. Abe bellowed at the top of his voice. The child was unhurt. Everyone had forgotten that Abe could still open his mouth. Perhaps he attached importance only to life that was still innocent, before it had been soiled by the pressures of society and the fragility of adults.

Perhaps he was saying to himself, in that infinite silence, that man, and especially a writer, does not have the strength to resist either the world's evil spells or his own demons.

Perhaps man's ultimate strength lies in silence. Yes, silence! Not the kind that comes from a recognition that one has nothing to say, or is incapable of expressing what one has to say. Neither retreat nor submissiveness. An active silence. For silence is active. It is an act. An energy that absorbs the world's beauty and rejects its ugliness. Perhaps the ultimate act, the most meaningful gesture, the most eloquent word, can be intensified only in silence.

Neither absence nor withdrawal. Oppose the din with silent music, answer idle talk with non-speech. Yes, silence. Irrevocable. Infinite silence.

For eighteen years Abraham M. Klein lived in his Outremont apartment, neither writing nor speaking. Friends came to see him, tried to get him to come out of his lair, out of his refuge. It was no use. His silence was total and permanent. Bessie and his children shared his life.

People on the outside, unfamiliar with the poet's life, thought his silence was the result of illness. No doubt. They might even be right. To reject the world may be an illness. A simple explanation, simplistic perhaps, and above all, reassuring.

For the poet who had taken part in human struggles, human joys, and human suffering, silence is probably the ultimate act of self-expression. Neither refusal nor condemnation. Expectation? Yes. Hope? Perhaps. The poet who does not reach the essential may go on his way, condemn himself to idle chatter, frivolous and useless noise.

Abe Klein had come close to that essential and had chosen silence – supreme silence and supreme self-expression.

And so, when he died in 1972, it was as if he were leaving on tiptoe, never to return.

National Archives of Canada/C-58355.

Klein introduces Pierre Van Paasen, a pro-Zionist writer, at a meeting in the Jewish Public Library in Montreal. Klein's commitment to his community and his country, instead of isolating him, opened the doors of the world.

# 9

## *Posterity*

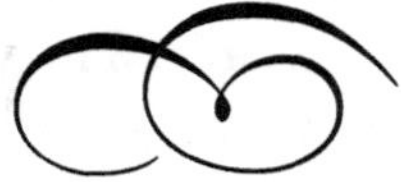

Long before Klein's death, commentaries and critical studies of his work had been appearing in increasing numbers. In English Canada, symposiums devoted to his writing were organized. Magazines published special numbers about him. Researchers gathered his articles and short stories into collections. At the universities, many doctoral dissertations and master's theses were written about his role as a writer and as a man.

Rarely has a man's life been so close to his work, and rarely has a work been so closely involved with a community, a country, an era. Klein's commitment to his community and his country, instead of isolating him, opened the doors of the world.

His city, Montreal, did not have closed boundaries. It was from his home, from his great metropolis, that he had access to humanity and to the universe at large.

As a poet, Klein was exacting and rigorous. But obeying the rules of the language in which he wrote did not prevent him from revising them. Like all creators, he was both the guardian of the traditions he had inherited and the founder of new traditions.

At the cost of internal conflicts and struggles against doubts and anguish, he had succeeded in reconciling his responsibilities as a man and a citizen with his commitment as a writer. He was immersed in his time, but through his writing he had lived beyond his time. Years after his death, his work maintains its importance and grows in influence. Its impact is still being calculated and its beauty discovered.

Poet, journalist, political activist, Klein accepted his origins, his era, and the diversity of his city and its culture. He was, and remains, a Jew, a Montrealer, a Quebecker, a Canadian. He was a man, *par excellence*.

# *Glossary*

**Bar-mitzvah**: a religious ceremony marking the rite of passage by which, at the age of thirteen, a young man considers himself a responsible member of the Jewish community.
**Halakah**: from the verb meaning "to walk." The body of written and oral laws (the Bible and the Mishnah) that govern Jewish life. They are unalterable, and are supplemented by subsequent rabbinical decisions made in accordance with the basic laws.
**Mitzvoth**: the body of commandments prescribed by the Torah, which Jews are obliged to observe. They number 613 in all, of which 365 are negative and 248 positive.
**Pesach**: the celebration of Passover, commemorating the escape of the Israelites from Egypt.
**Phylacteries**: small boxes containing quotations from the Torah, which a religious Jew ties around his forehead and left arm in a ritual manner, by means of straps, at the time of certain prayers and, especially, every morning.
**Purim**: festival commemorating the saving of the Jews threatened with extermination by Haman, an adviser to

the Persian King Ahasuerus. Thanks to the determination of Mordecai and his niece, Queen Esther, Haman was exposed and condemned.
**Shabbat**: the Jewish Sabbath.
**Shavuoth**: the weeks between Passover and Pentecost (the Jewish harvest festival).
**Shoah**: genocide of the Jews by the Nazis during World War II, which claimed six million victims. Sometimes referred to as the Holocaust.
**Shofar**: a ram's horn used in the synagogue on New Year's Day and Yom Kippur. The sounding of the shofar announces the end of the fast.
**Sukkoth**: Festival of Tabernacles commemorating the forty years that the Jewish people spent in the desert before entering the Promised Land.
**Talmud Torah**: a Jewish parochial school for teaching Hebrew, Bible, Jewish history, and the rudiments of Jewish religion and culture.
**Tefillin**: *see* Phylacteries.
**Yarmulke**: a skullcap worn by Jewish men.
**Yahrzeit**: a memorial marking the date of someone's death.
**YHVH**: a divine tetragram not to be pronounced by man. It is sometimes written as YAHWEH.
**Yiddish**: the everyday language spoken by Jews in or from Central and Eastern Europe. Yiddish was derived from medieval German, contains elements of Hebrew and the Slavic languages, and is written in Hebrew characters.
**Zionist**: someone who supported Zionism, the worldwide Jewish movement for the establishment in Palestine of a national homeland for the Jews, or who today supports the development of the Jewish nation in Israel.

National Archives of Canada/PA-125749.

Abraham Moses Klein
Years after his death, his writing maintains its importance and grows in influence. Its impact is still being calculated and its beauty discovered.

# *Chronology of A.M. Klein (1909-1972)*

*Compiled by Michèle Vanasse*

| Klein and His Times | Canada and the World |
|---|---|
| **1880**<br>After a series of pogroms, the Jews of Central Europe begin leaving for the west. | |
| | **1894**<br>Beginning of the Dreyfus affair in France. A Jewish officer, unjustly convicted of espionage, is sent to a penal colony. |
| | **1896**<br>The Jewish Hungarian writer Theodor Herzl publishes *Der Judenstaat* (*The Jewish State*), setting forth the idea of settling Jews in Palestine, then under Ottoman rule. This book laid the foundation of Zionism, the Jewish nationalist movement advocating the establishment of a Jewish state in Israel. |

| Klein and His Times | Canada and the World |
|---|---|
| **1897**<br>Lyon Cohen founds the first Jewish periodical in Canada, *The Jewish Times*, which reacts to the anti-Semitism aroused by the controversy over the Dreyfus affair. | |
| **1898**<br>The first Zionist organization in Canada, the Agudath Zion, is founded. | **1898**<br>The United States intervenes in the war between Spain and Cuba. Cuba becomes independent under American trusteeship. This serves the interests of the financiers. The independence of Cuba marks the end of the Spanish empire in America. |
| | **1900**<br>*The Protocols of the Elders of Zion*, a document intended to discredit the Jews, is published in Russia. |
| **1903**<br>The Quebec provincial legislature rules on the status of Jewish children in the Protestant schools. They are to be treated in the same way as Protestants, having the same obligations and the same rights. Poalei Zion, the largest organization speaking for the Zionist movement, is founded. | |
| | **1905**<br>In Russia, the Tsar is forced to recall the Duma, an elected consultative assembly, in the face of workers' strikes and peasant revolts. |

**KLEIN AND HIS TIMES**

**1906**
The first Yiddish book to be published in Canada, *Education among the Jews*, by E. Lewine, is published in Montreal.

**1907**
The Yiddish daily *Kanader Adler* is founded in Montreal. It sets itself the task of informing new immigrants about the history and political life of their new country.

**1909**
Birth of Abraham Moses Klein. Some accounts say he was born in Ratno, Ukraine.

**1910**
The Klein family arrives in Canada and settles on Saint-Charles-Borromée St., in the southern part of the Jewish immigrant quarter, which extends on both sides of St. Lawrence Blvd. from the St. Lawrence River to Duluth St.

**1914**
Klein enters elementary school at Mount Royal School, which he will attend until 1922. After school and on Saturdays, he also goes to the Talmud Torah school, financed by the community, for his religious education.

**CANADA AND THE WORLD**

**1913**
Twenty thousand Jewish immigrants arrive in Canada.

**1914**
World War I begins. A Serbian terrorist assassinates the heir to the Austrian throne, Archduke Francis Ferdinand, in Sarajevo and sets off a world conflict because of the network of alliances. Austria and Germany are allied against Russia, France, and Great Britain. Canada takes part in

**Klein and His Times**

*The Canadian Jewish Chronicle* begins publishing in Montreal.

The Jewish Library, a popular centre of secular Jewish culture, opens in Montreal.

**1919**

The Canadian Jewish Congress is founded for the purpose of defending the interests of Canadian Jews and cooperating with other Jewish congresses throughout the world.

**Canada and the World**

the war because Parliament believes it must support the cause of the British Empire.

**1917**

The Canadian Parliament votes for conscription. Quebec's opposition to this causes a rift in national unity. In Great Britain, the Balfour Declaration favours a national homeland for the Jews in Palestine, a land inhabited by Arabs.

**1918**

An armistice is signed on 11 November. The cost of war has been tragic: at least thirteen million dead, widespread destruction, especially in the Balkans, Poland, and France. In addition, an epidemic of Spanish influenza takes more than a million lives.

**1919**

Prohibition in the United States. A ban on the sale of alcoholic beverages encourages the development of smuggling and crime by bootleggers such as Al Capone.

The Treaty of Versailles redraws the map of central Europe and the Balkans. Yugoslavia is created from the states of Serbia, Croatia, Slovenia, and Montenegro.

**KLEIN AND HIS TIMES**

**1920**
First collection of poems by J.L. Segal is published.

**1922**
Abraham Klein enters Baron Byng High School.

**CANADA AND THE WORLD**

**1920**
Beginning of the "roaring twenties" in the United States, years of post-war prosperity until the crash of 1929. This period sees the development of an American lifestyle characterized by the possession of material goods that make life more comfortable (cars, radios, kitchen utensils).

Jewish colonists settle in Palestine, now under British mandate. There are many clashes with the local population.

**1921**
The Canadian Catholic Federation of Labour, a trade union movement which will later become the Confederation of National Unions, is founded.

Ireland is divided into two parts: the Catholic Irish Free State, and Ulster, with a Protestant majority, which remains an integral part of the United Kingdom.

In China, the Chinese Communist Party is founded. Mao Zedong is one of the founders.

**1922**
Benito Mussolini, *Il Duce*, the leader of the Italian Fascists, forms a new government with full powers. Fascism is a nationalist and totalitarian philosophy, opposed to socialism. The Congress of Soviets founds the Union of Soviet Socialist Republics.

**KLEIN AND HIS TIMES**

**1923**
In Montreal, thirty-two Jewish organizations announce their support for a separate Jewish school.

**1924**
Klein and some friends form a small intellectual circle, called the Shalom Aleichem Club, to discuss modern Yiddish literature. He meets David Lewis, who will become one of his closest friends.

**1926**
Klein enrolls in political science and economics at McGill University. He joins Young Judaea, an organization of young Zionists. He believes that Israel should be a political refuge for the Jewish people, but especially a spiritual centre stimulating a rebirth of Jewish creativity throughout the world.

Klein also takes part in many debates at the university, along with David Lewis. Zionism, Judaism, and socialism are burning issues. He joins a group of poets, known as the Montreal Group, which includes Arthur Smith, Frank Scott, Leo Kennedy, and Leon Edel, all of them early members of a modernist movement in English literature.

**1927**
Klein publishes poems and humorous essays in *The McGill Daily*, signed AMK. He also publishes a

**CANADA AND THE WORLD**

**1926**
W.L. Mackenzie King becomes the Liberal prime minister of Canada. He will be in power until 1930, and again from 1935 to 1948.

**1927**
The American pilot Charles Lindbergh makes the first solo transatlantic nonstop flight from

**KLEIN AND HIS TIMES**

poem in the New York *Menorah Journal*.

**1928**
Klein becomes editor-in-chief of *The Judaean*, and writes political and social articles, as well as poetry, for *The McGill Daily*.

**1930**
With his friend David Lewis, Klein launches a new magazine on campus, *The McGilliad*. In the fall he begins studying law at the University of Montreal, because he wants to speak fluent French in order to facilitate the practice of his profession in Quebec.

**1931**
Ninety-four per cent of the Jews living in Quebec list Yiddish as their mother tongue.

**CANADA AND THE WORLD**

New York to Paris, covering 5,800 kilometres in 33 hours, 30 minutes.

*The Jazz Singer* is the first talking movie to appear on the screen.

**1929**
On "Black Thursday," 24 October, the New York Stock Exchange collapses. It is the Wall Street crash.

**1931**
The Statute of Westminster confirms Canada's independence from Great Britain in national and international affairs.

In Great Britain, the Statute of Westminster institutionalizes the British Empire. The Commonwealth is made up of a group of independent countries including the United Kingdom, Canada, Australia, the Union of South Africa, the Irish Free State, and India.

**Klein and His Times**

**1932**
Klein collects 150 of his poems, written since the mid-twenties, in *Gestures Hebraic* and *Poems*. They are not published, but Leon Edel, to whom Klein showed them, wrote an article in *The Canadian Forum*.

**1933**
Kalman Klein, the father of Abraham Klein, dies, leaving no estate. Abe assumes financial responsibility for the family.

In Montreal, Toronto, and Winnipeg, public protests are held against the persecution of the Jews in Germany by the Nazis. The Canadian Jewish Congress launches a campaign to raise funds to help Jewish refugees and to fight anti-Semitic propaganda.

**1934**
Klein and his partner, Max Garmaise, open a law office at the corner of Bleury and Sainte-Catherine Streets. Klein becomes national president of Young Judaea.

The Montreal Jewish General Hospital is founded.

**Canada and the World**

**1932**
In Canada, new political parties offer solutions to the economic crisis: the Co-operative Commonwealth Federation (CCF), founded by James Woodsworth, and Social Credit, founded by William Aberhart.

In the United States, the Democratic president, Franklin D. Roosevelt, offers the New Deal, a policy of recovery favouring state intervention in the economy in order to provide a more equitable distribution of goods.

**1933**
Rise of the National Socialist (Nazi) party in Germany, a totalitarian party that holds democrats, Jews, and Marxists responsible for Germany's ills. This philosophy is based on racism, preaches the superiority of the Aryan race, and demands total obedience of its members to one leader, Adolf Hitler.

**1934**
In Germany, Hitler (the *Führer*) becomes absolute leader of the army and the country.

German Jews begin to flee to other European countries.

| **Klein and His Times** | **Canada and the World** |
|---|---|
| **1935**<br>Klein and Bessie Kozlov are married. | |
| **1936**<br>Klein is increasingly active in the Zionist Organization of Canada and becomes editor-in-chief and publicity director for the monthly *Canadian Zionist*.<br><br>Ecumenical meetings are held in Montreal between Jesuits, lay persons, and Jews. | **1936**<br>A political reorganization begins in Quebec. Preaching economic and social liberation of French Canadians from the big private companies, often foreign-owned, Paul Gouin founds the Action Libérale Nationale (ALN). Maurice Duplessis, leader of the Conservative Party, unites with the ALN to create the Union Nationale, which wins the election.<br><br>Hitlerite Germany and Fascist Italy form an alliance.<br><br>Civil war breaks out in Spain between the extreme-right nationalists of General Franco and the Republicans. Franco is victorious in 1939.<br><br>In the U.S.S.R., the Bolshevik Old Guard is liquidated by Stalin. |
| **1937**<br>Birth of Abraham's first son, Colman. The family moves to Rouyn, in the Abitibi region, where Max Garmaise and Klein open a new office. | |
| **1938**<br>Klein and his family return to Montreal, where he accepts a new position as editor-in-chief of *The Canadian Jewish Chronicle*. | |

**KLEIN AND HIS TIMES**

*Canada's Jews*, by Louis Rosenberg, an exhaustive demographic analysis based on data from the 1931 census, is published.

**1939**
Samuel Bronfman, the newly elected president of the Canadian Jewish Congress, invites Klein to be his public relations consultant.

**1940**
Klein's first collection of poetry, *Hath Not a Jew*, is published.

**1941**
Klein's second son, Sandor, is born.

**CANADA AND THE WORLD**

**1939**
World War II breaks out. The German invasion of Poland causes France and Great Britain to declare war on Germany and, in 1940, on her Italian ally.

In Quebec, the Liberal Party under Adélard Godbout is returned to power.

Canada declares war on Germany.

The United States remains neutral in the world conflict, but supplies armaments to the Allies.

**1940**
In Quebec, women are granted the right to vote.

France capitulates. General Charles de Gaulle calls on the French to resist Germany and forms the Free French Forces.

**1941**
Germany invades the U.S.S.R.

Japan attacks the U.S. naval base at Pearl Harbor, Hawaii. The Americans declare war on Japan. Germany and Italy declare war on the United States.

**Klein and His Times**

**1942**
Klein joins a group of poets who publish their work in two literary journals, *Preview* and *First Statement*, between 1942 and 1945.

**1944**
Klein's poem *The Hitleriad*, which denounces Adolf Hitler and praises Winston Churchill, is published.

Klein accepts the CCF nomination in the constituency of Cartier, but withdraws before the election of 1945.

**1945**
Through the influence of Samuel Bronfman, Klein is appointed a lecturer in English literature at McGill University until 1948.

His daughter Sharon is born.

*History of the Jews in Canada*, by B.G. Sack, is published in Montreal.

**Canada and the World**

**1942**
In Canada, Prime Minister Mackenzie King calls a plebiscite on conscription. The vote is 63 per cent in favour in Canada as a whole, and 71.2 per cent against in Quebec. The anti-conscriptionists found the Bloc Populaire. André Laurendeau becomes its provincial leader in 1944.

**1944**
In Quebec, Duplessis returns to power and remains in office until 1959. His political philosophy is based on traditional values: land, work, family, and the church. It does not encourage social legislation and opposes the organized labour movement (e.g., the miners' strike at Asbestos in 1949).

The CCF is elected in Saskatchewan.

**1945**
The United States drops the first atomic bomb on Hiroshima, Japan. The war ends. Germany has been crushed with tremendous losses. More than sixty million people have been killed, nine million of them (including six million Jews) in concentration camps.

Jean-Paul Sartre and Albert Camus dominate the intellectual scene, Roberto Rossellini and Vittorio De Sica the cinema.

| **Klein and His Times** | **Canada and the World** |
|---|---|
| | The United Nations organization (UN) is founded. Its role is to maintain peace in the world and to protect the fundamental rights of man. |
| **1946**<br>Klein writes a spy novel, *That Walks Like a Man*, which is never published. | |
| | **1947**<br>Canada is a member of the UN. Thousands of Jewish survivors of the war in Europe are admitted to the country. |
| **1948**<br>Klein's collection of poetry, *The Rocking Chair*, is published. | **1948**<br>A Jewish state is created in Palestine and its independence proclaimed. Open war begins between Israelis and Arabs. |
| **1949**<br>Klein runs again as a CCF candidate in the June federal election, but is defeated and retires from political activity. In August he is sent by the Canadian Jewish Congress to Israel, Europe, and North Africa to study the problem of the Jewish refugees. He also writes reports for *The Canadian Jewish Chronicle*. On his return, he will spend three years travelling across Canada and the United States, giving lectures about Israel. | **1949**<br>Canada is a member of the North Atlantic Treaty Organization (NATO), set up to defend the free world.<br><br>In China, Mao proclaims the People's Republic of China. |
| **1950**<br>The Jewish community begins to open its doors to the French lan- | **1950**<br>The United States, under President Dwight D. Eisenhower, |

| **Klein and His Times** | **Canada and the World** |
|---|---|
| guage, by the creation, among other things, of the Cercle Juif de Langue Française. The proportion of Yiddish speakers will fall from 95 per cent to 25 per cent, and English becomes the common language of Jewish institutions. | intervenes when Communist North Korea attacks South Korea. |
| **1951**<br>Klein's novel, *The Second Scroll*, is published. | |
| **1952**<br>At the request of Samuel Bronfman, Klein writes a history of the Canadian Jewish Congress, but his manuscript is not accepted. | **1952**<br>First television broadcasts in Canada. |
| | **1953**<br>Stalin dies. Nikita Khrushchev becomes general secretary of the Soviet Communist Party. |
| **1954**<br>Klein gives up almost all his activities and leads a more and more cloistered life at home, suffering from depression, the cause and nature of which are still a mystery today. | |
| | **1955**<br>The countries of Eastern Europe form a military alliance known as the Warsaw Pact. |
| **1956**<br>Immigration of French-speaking Sephardic Jews (those from Mediterranean countries) to Quebec begins. | **1956**<br>An uprising in Hungary is put down by Soviet intervention. |

**Klein and His Times**

**Canada and the World**

**1957**
In Canada, Lester B. Pearson wins the Nobel Peace Prize. As Canada's representative at the UN, he had suggested sending a peacekeeping force to the Suez Canal region in Egypt to restore order.

The European Economic Community (EEC) is created with a view to preserving Europe's identity vis-a-vis the two great powers, the U.S.S.R. and the U.S., by electing a parliament and adopting a common economic policy.

**1959**
In Canada, the St. Lawrence Seaway is opened.

In Cuba, Fidel Castro leads a successful socialist revolution

**1960**
In Quebec, the Liberal Party, led by Jean Lesage, begins the "Quiet Revolution," a vast program of social and economic reforms: hospitalization insurance in 1961, nationalization of hydroelectric power (the favourite theme of natural resources minister René Lévesque) in 1962, school reform in 1965.

**1961**
In Canada, the CCF becomes the New Democratic Party (NDP).

The Jewish population of Canada reaches 254,368.

| KLEIN AND HIS TIMES | CANADA AND THE WORLD |
|---|---|
| | John F. Kennedy becomes president of the United States. The country becomes involved in the war between Communist North Vietnam and South Vietnam. |
| | Soviet cosmonaut Yuri Gagarin becomes the first person to orbit the earth. |
| **1962**<br>In Montreal, the Protestant School Board recommends to the Royal Commission on Education that the Jewish School Commission be restored. | **1962**<br>U.S. astronaut John Glenn becomes the first American to orbit the earth. |
| | Under pressure from the United States, the U.S.S.R. stops sending military aid to Cuba. The peaceful settlement of the Cuban Missile crisis furthers the detente between East and West. |
| | **1963**<br>In the United States, President John F. Kennedy is assassinated in Dallas, Texas. Under his successor, Lyndon B. Johnson, the military buildup in Vietnam continues. |
| **1965**<br>Massive immigration of Sephardic Jews from North Africa. | |
| | **1966**<br>In Quebec, Daniel Johnson, leader of the Union Nationale, becomes premier. |
| | In the United States, the Civil Rights Bill is adopted by Congress to eliminate racial segregation in |

**KLEIN AND HIS TIMES**

**CANADA AND THE WORLD**

schools, public places, the workplace, and the political arena.

Young Americans protest against the war in Vietnam, advocating love and nonviolence. "Flower-power" hippies experiment with new lifestyles based on communal living and freedom from taboos.

In China, Mao launches the cultural revolution.

**1967**
As part of Canada's centennial celebrations, Expo 67, a world exhibition, is held in Montreal. During his visit, French President Charles de Gaulle utters his famous words, "*Vive le Québec libre.*"

The preliminary report of the Royal Commission on Bilingualism and Biculturalism is published. The government of Canada makes an effort to promote bilingualism in the civil service.

**1968**
The Quebec legislature passes a law on private educational institutions and subsidies are granted to private Jewish schools

**1968**
In Quebec, the Parti Québécois is launched by René Lévesque.

In the United States, the black pastor Martin Luther King, an advocate of nonviolence, and Robert Kennedy, the candidate of the minorities, are assassinated.

There is worldwide student unrest; in France it breaks the power of de Gaulle.

| **Klein and His Times** | **Canada and the World** |
|---|---|
| | In Czechoslovakia, the intervention of Warsaw Pact troops in Prague ends the Czech people's hopes of freeing themselves from the Soviet yoke. |
| | **1969**<br>The American astronauts Neil Armstrong and Edwin Aldrin are the first men to walk on the moon. |
| **1971**<br>Death of Abraham Klein's wife, Bessie. | |
| **1972**<br>Death of Abraham Klein after eighteen years of seclusion and silence. | |
| | **1973**<br>The Americans withdraw from Vietnam. |
| **1976**<br>*Adieu Babylone*, by Naïm Kattan, is published. | |

# *Recommended Reading*

**Books by A.M. Klein:**

*The Second Scroll.* New York: Alfred A. Knopf, 1951. Canadian edition: Toronto: McClelland and Stewart, 1961.

*The Rocking Chair.* Toronto: Ryerson, 1948.

*The Hitleriad.* New York: New Directions, 1944.

*Poems*, Philadelphia: The Jewish Publication Society of America, 1944.

*Hath Not a Jew.* New York: Behrman House Inc., 1940. Preface by Ludwig Lewisohn.

*New Provinces.* Toronto: MacMillan, 1930. Two poems: "Out of the Pulver and the Polished Lens" and "Soirée of Velvel Kleinburger."

# Index

www.ingramcontent.com/pod-product-compliance
Lightning Source LLC
LaVergne TN
LVHW051839080426
835512LV00018B/2966

* 9 7 8 0 9 6 8 8 1 6 6 6 0 *